The Royal Navy's Revenge and Other Little-known Encounters of the War at Sea

A painting of the Thai coast defense ship Dhonburi *under French fire during the battle. of Koh Chang 1941.*

Vincent P. O'Hara

Nimble Books LLC

Nimble Books LLC

1521 Martha Avenue

Ann Arbor, MI, USA 48103

http://www.NimbleBooks.com

wfz@nimblebooks.com

+1.734-330-2593

Version 1.0; last saved 2013-04-30.

Printed in the United States of America

ISBN-13: 978-1-60888-113-0

The paper used in this publication meets the minimum requirements of the American National Standard for Information Sciences—Permanence of Paper for Printed Library Materials, ANSI Z39.48-1992. The paper is acid-free and lignin-free.

CONTENTS

Preface and Acknowledgements iv

Chapter 1. The Battle of Koh Chang 1

Chapter 2. Attack and Sink! The Italian Victory off Bastia Harbor: 9 September 1943 15

Chapter 3. The Royal Navy's Revenge: The Battle of Penang Strait, 16 May 1945 32

Chapter 4. Defiant Until the End: The Naval Campaign in the Channel Islands 47

Chapter 5. Mystery Battle off Imperia, 1 October 1944 67

Chapter 6. The Naval War off Syria: The Royal Navy fights the Marine Nationale, June 1941 79

Chapter 7. The Road Back Began At Balikpapan 96

Bibliography 110

NIMBLE BOOKS LLC

PREFACE AND ACKNOWLEDGEMENTS

The articles in this collection appeared between 2004 and 2008 in *World War II, Tin Can Sailor*, and *Pacific War/World War Two Quarterly*. In addition there is one article that has never been published. They all describe naval actions that have been lost in the shuffle of more famous, although sometimes less interesting events.

The presentation here does not attempt to replicate the layout of the original articles, although it does include many of the same illustrations and maps. I have taken the opportunity to make an occasional correction, and I have tried to apply a coherent style but otherwise, the material is as originally written. With the exception of the action against *Haguro*, which is the subject matter of this book's title article, and Koh Chang, all of these actions have been described in my books, but in a much abbreviated form. In some cases, the article allowed me to present new material which came to light after the book was published. The Mystery Battle off Imperia is a good example. An eyewitness to the battle contacted me a year after the publication of the *German Fleet at War* and described what he had seen at night. In the case of *Defiant until the End* I was helped by a Polish gentleman in tracking down and translating accounts of the Polish warship that participated in the campaign.

There are several people I would like to acknowledge and thank. First, Fred Zimmerman, the publisher of Nimble Books, for giving such material a second life and making it available to a new audience. My thanks go to the editors who originally accepted and published these articles: Christopher J. Anderson, Robert von Maier, and Terry Miller. A special thanks goes to Richard Latture, the editor of *Naval History* magazine who agreed to release Koh Chang from his story bank for publication in this book. Enrico Cernuschi and Przemyslaw Federowicz provided information otherwise unavailable to me. Finally and most importantly, I thank my wife, Maria and my children, Yunuen and Vincent for giving their husband and father the space and support to pursue his interests in naval history.

CHAPTER 1. THE BATTLE OF KOH CHANG

INTRODUCTION

"After an hour and forty minutes of continuous combat, several enemy ships lay at the bottom, their locations marked only by columns of black smoke in the deserted roads."[1] This is how Captain R. Berenger of the French cruiser *Lamotte-Picquet* described his engagement with the Royal Thai Navy at Koh Chang, a coastal island in the Gulf of Siam near the French Indo-Chinese and Thai border. He claimed complete destruction of the enemy force of two 8-inch coastal cruisers and three small destroyers. This news came as a heady tonic seven months after France's defeat by the Germans, at a time when the nation's morale was at low ebb, and it has been proclaimed as France's greatest naval victory of World War II, inflicting on the enemy "a defeat as decisive in is way as the Japanese at Tsushima."[2] This was the contemporary assessment and for sixty years it has prevailed. But is it accurate?

The Battle of Koh Chang, the only naval action of the short Franco-Thai border war of 1940–41, occurred on 17 January 1941. Western accounts are based upon French reports. Not surprisingly, these reports contain inaccuracies. Thai accounts are less accessible and the official record of the battle is still classified. However, Koh Chang was the Royal Thai Navy's most important action and it has studied this action extensively. The Thai record contradicts the French as to the number of ships engaged, the damage inflicted, and most importantly, the battle's ultimate impact.

It is time for a reassessment of Koh Chang.

---

[1] *La bataille de Koh Chang.* Report of 18 January 1941.
[2] Manley, "Koh Chang."

Figure 1. Overview of the battle of Koh Chang (V. P. O'Hara)

Hɪꜱᴛᴏʀɪᴄᴀʟ Bᴀᴄᴋɢʀᴏᴜɴᴅ

China, Japan and Thailand were the only East Asian nations never co-lonized by a European power, but in the case of Thailand, it was a near thing, and preserving independence cost the country nearly half its territo-ry. Thailand's relationship with France was particularly difficult. Paris ex-panded its Indo-Chinese colony at the expense of Siam's eastern provinces and protectorates, annexing portions of Cambodia in 1867, portions of Laos in 1888, 1893, and 1904 and the balance of Cambodia in 1907.[3] The Franco-Siamese crisis of 1893 was particularly traumatic. Siam's modern navy fired its first shots against a foreign foe on 13 July 1893, resisting a classic case of gunboat diplomacy when the French warships *Inconstant*

---

[3] The Kingdom of Siam became the Kingdom of Thailand in 1939. The Kingdom is referred to as Siam before that date and Thailand thereafter.

and *Comete* forced the forts at Pakham below Bangkok and imposed territorial and political concessions on the government.

Given this history, it is not surprising that Thailand closely observed the misfortunes France suffered in the spring of 1940. The concessions gained by Japan encouraged the Kingdom to press for concessions of its own. Bangkok wanted France to return potions of the territories taken thirty years before in 1904 and 1907. On 14 October the Vichy government refused, citing, among other reasons, the non-aggression pact France had signed with Thailand on 12 June of that year. In November the Thai army began probing French positions along the Cambodian and Laotian frontiers. On 10 January 1941 Thailand invaded French Indo-China with six battalions at two points in Laos and sixteen battalions at three points in Cambodia.

The French did not seriously contest the Laotian incursions, but the fifteen French battalions available in Cambodia nearly equaled the invaders in strength. Despite this parity, the Thai central force captured Piopet and advanced toward Sisophen nearly fifty kilometers into Cambodia. The French massed four battalions and some armor and artillery and planned a counteroffensive. On the morning of 16 January they attacked the Thai spearheads from northwest of Sisophen. In a daylong battle, the Thais thoroughly defeated this French ""*masse de maneuvre*.""

THE NAVAL FORCES

Rear Admiral Jules Terraux commanded French naval forces in Indo-China. In addition to river gunboats and auxiliaries, Terraux could deploy five warships for operations against Thailand: the light cruiser *Lamotte-Picquet* (7,249 tons; eight 6.1-inch and four 3-inch dual purpose [DP] guns; twelve 21.7-inch torpedo tubes; 33 knots; 1926), the large colonial sloops *Dumont d'Urbville* and *Amiral Charner* (1,970 tons; three 5.45-inch guns; 15.5 knots; 1932) and the World War I era gunboats *Marne* (600 tons; four 3.9-inch guns; 21 knots; 1916) and *Tahure* (850 tons; two 5.45-inch guns, 21 knots; 1918). On 9 December 1940 he formed these vessels into the *Groupe Occasionnel* under Captain R. Berenger, a long-time veteran of the eastern station, former skipper of *Marne* and captain of *Lamotte-Picquet*. This flotilla trained at Cam Ranh Bay and waited a call to action.

Figure 2. A modern "colonial" sloop of the *Bougainville* class. These warships were designed to serve in overseas stations and uphold French imperial interests. She carried three 5.5-inch/40 guns. (Storia Militare)

Figure 3. The light cruiser *Lamotte-Picquet* was the flagship of the French Indochinese squadron. She was laid down in 1923 and carried eight 6.1-inch guns as well as a dozen 21.7-inch torpedo tubes. U.S. Navy aircraft sank her off Saigon in January 1945. (Storia Militare)

The Royal Thai Navy was a recently modernized force and one with considerable regional potential. It acquired its first steam warships, a corvette and four gunboats, from France in 1865. It was, at one point, commanded by a Dane, Admiral Andreas de Richelieu, and many officers were Danish or Norwegian. In some respects it was modeled after the Scandinavian navies with small but heavily armed coast defense ships supported by small, fast torpedo boats and coastal submarines.

In January 1941 the Royal Thai Navy included:

- Two coast defense ships, *Dhonburi* and *Sri Ayuthia*: (2,265 tons; four 8-inch, four 3-inch DP guns; 15.5 knots; 1938).

- Two armored gun-boats, *Ratanakosindra* and *Sukhothai* (861 tons; four 6-inch, four 3-inch DP guns; 12 knots; 1925 and 1930).

- Two sloops, *Tachin* and *Meklong* (1,400 tons; four 4.7-inch guns; four 21-inch torpedo tubes; 17 knots; 1936 and 1937).

- Four submarines, *Sinsamudar*, *Vilun*, *Machanu*, and *Blajunbol* (370/430 tons surfaced/submerged; one 3-inch DP gun; five 24-inch torpedo tubes, 14.5/8 knots surfaced/submerged; 1938).

- One destroyer/training ship, *Phra Ruang* (1,035 tons; three 4-inch, one 3-inch DP guns; four 21-inch torpedo tubes; 35 knots; 1917).

- One gunboat, *Chow Phraya* (840 tons; two 3-inch guns; 16 knots; 1918).

- Nine torpedo boats, *Chandraburi*, *Chonburi*, *Chunphorn*, *Patani*, *Puket*, *Rayong*, *Songhkli*, *Surasdra*, and *Trad* (318 tons; three 3-inch DP guns; six 17.7-inch torpedo tubes; 31 knots; 1935-38).

- Three small torpedo boats, *Kantan*, *Takbai* and *Kylongyai* (110 tons; one 3-inch DP gun; two 18-inch torpedo tubes; 19 knots; 1937).

- Two minelayers, *Bangrachan* and *Nhongarhai* (368 tons; two 3-inch DP guns; 142 mines; 13 knots; 1936)

- Nine motor torpedo boats, *1-5* (11 tons; two 17.7-inch torpedo tubes; 37 knots) and *6-9* (16 tons; two 17.7-inch torpedo tubes; 40 knots).

Figure 4. *Dhonburi* underway prewar with her crew dressing the rails. (Storia Militare)

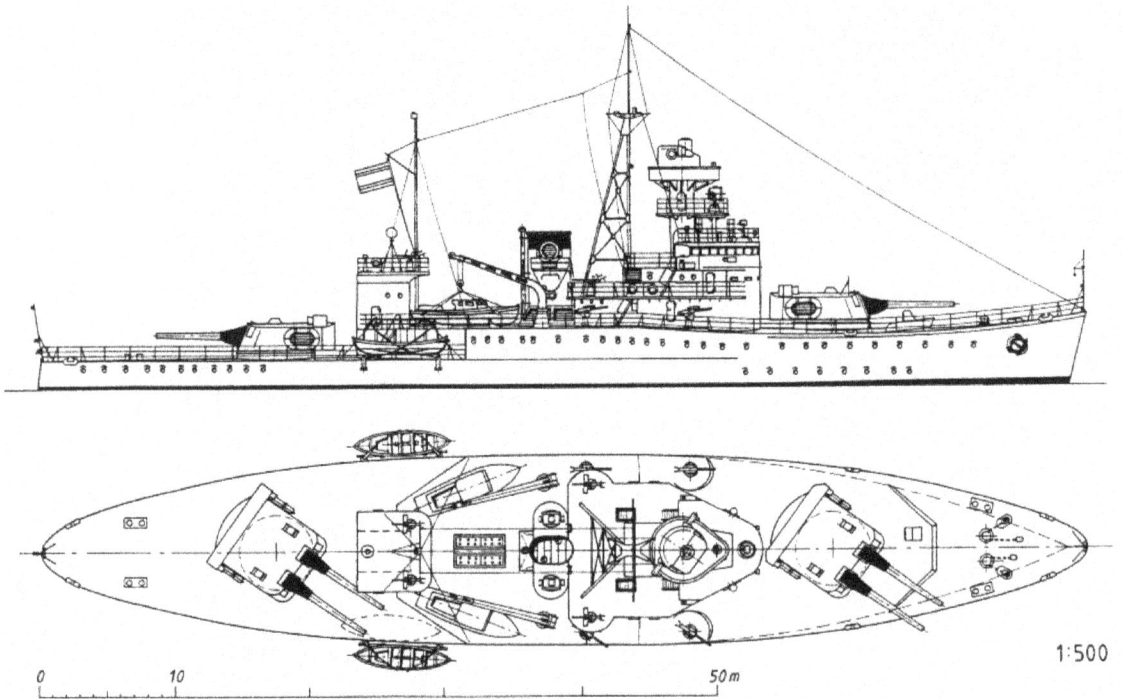

Figure 5. *Dhonburi* constructed in Japan and armed with 8-inch guns, Dhonburi was an innovative design and unlike any other modern vessel in service at the time. Her concept was similar to the coastal battleships of the late 19th and early 20th centuries. (source unknown)

THE CAMPAIGN

On 1 December 1940 Thai naval headquarters dispatched a powerful flotilla consisting of its two coastal defense ships, *Dhonburi* and *Sri Ayudhaya*, four submarines, three torpedo boats, *Trad*, *Phuket*, and *Surat Thani*, and the minelayer *Bangrachan* to patrol the waters around Koh Chang and guard against a French incursion. The coast defense ships landed a detachment of marines on the mainland at Laem Ngop, just north of Koh Chang on the 2nd. Then faults in her hydraulic system forced *Sri Ayudhaya* to return to Bangkok on 6 December. The balance of the surface force followed on the 10th.

The task of protecting the Thai maritime flank fell to the submarines until 1 January 1941. On this date Naval Headquarters ordered the First Squadron forward from Bangkok to Sattahip. This force was commanded by Luang Sangwonyutthakit and consisted of *Sri Ayudhaya* (flag), the torpedo boats *Surat Thani*, *Pkuket*, *Trad* and the minelayer *Bang Rachan,* and the Second Squadron with the armored gunboat *Sukothai*, torpedo boat *Chumporn*, and sloops *Tachin* and *Maeklong*.. However, mechanical difficulties quickly forced *Sukothai*, *Maeklong*, *Trad*, and *Chumporn* to return to Bangkok. The balance of the force maintained its forward deployment while the Third Squadron, under Luang Promwiraphanand and consisting of *Dhonburi*, (flag), the torpedo boats *Songkla*, *Chonburi*, and *Rayong*, and the minelayer *Nongsarai* rotated forward to Sattahip to replace the vessels that had returned to Bangkok.

On 13 January the commander of the French army requested a naval action to support the ground offensive planned for 16 January near Sisophen. Captain Berenger met with Rear Admiral Terraux, the governor general, Admiral Jean Decoux, and the army command in Saigon where they finalized their plan. They gave Berenger discretion to attack according to the situation and Thai dispositions. The sloops and gunboats sailed from Cam Ranh Bay at 1600 on 15 January. Berenger, aboard *Lamotte-Picquet*, refueled his ship at Saigon and caught up with the others that evening.

The French flotilla sailed from the anchorage of Poulo Condore at 2100 on 15 January. The next day they entered the Gulf of Siam sailing at 13.5 knots, the best speed of the two colonial sloops. Although the Thai air force had reconnaissance units deployed in the area, they failed to detect the enemy's approach. French reconnaissance, however, reported that the Thai fleet was divided into two formations, one based at the mainland port of Sattahib and another at the roads of Koh Chang, the northernmost island in a small archipelago twenty miles off the coast near the Thai-Cambodian frontier. Berenger decided to attack Koh Chang because it was the nearer target and lacked Sattahib's fortifications.

The Thai force the French spotted at Koh Chang on 15 January consisted of the First Squadron: *Sri Ayudhaya* with two torpedo boats, a sloop and a minelayer. However, this was just before the Third Squadron relieved the First, which departed the area that night and arrived back at Sattahip on 16 January.

The anchorage, located at the southern end of Koh Chang Island, had three exits defined by small islands further offshore. Berenger timed his approach to arrive at 0530, an hour and a quarter before dawn. At 0545 he divided his force into three divisions to cover each of the exits: the cruiser acting alone to the east of Koh Klum, the sloops in the center between Koh Kra and Koh Klum, and the gunboats to the west between Koh Kra and Koh Chang. He intended to commence action at 0615.

At 0605 a Loire 130 seaplane based at Ream flew over the anchorage for a final look and reported that two coastal defense ships and three torpedo boats were anchored there. The plane then attempted to attack, but a heavy anti-air barrage drove it off. Its report was inaccurate. In fact the Thai Third Squadron was considerably dispersed. The torpedo boats *Chonburi* and *Songkla* lay at the anchorage, *Dhonburi*, the minelayer *Nongsarai*, and the fishery protection vessel *Theiw Uthok* were at the island's eastern side well north of the anchorage, while the torpedo boat *Rayong* had been patrolling to the east that night and was anchored near Koh Kut, southeast of Koh Chang, twenty-five kilometers away. *Sri Ayudahaya* was at Sattahip, nearly two hundred kilometers away.

THE BATTLE

The Loire's report surprised Berenger; he now expected both of the heavy coast defense ships, a force stronger than he had intended to engage. However, he did not attempt to revise his plan and action commenced as scheduled. As dawn approached conditions favored battle: the sea was flat, the air calm; there was a heavy overcast and light ground fog, although visibility was otherwise good. The French report asserts that *Chonburi* and *Songkla* opened fire first on *Dumont d'Urbville* and *Amiral Charner*, which were silhouetted against a clear horizon and a setting moon. Hidden by ground mist and the dark mass of the island, the torpedo boats began the lengthy process of raising steam. The French colonial sloops returned fire from nine thousand meters, ranging on the muzzle flashes of their foe.[4] They were almost due south of Koh Kram, which was situated six kilometers southwest of the anchorage. Their initial salvos were long, but reportedly destroyed a Thai shore observation post. *Marne* and *Tahure* were thirteen kilometers west, southwest while *Lamotte-Piquet* was sailing east at twenty-two knots temporarily screened by Koh Klum, the island seven kilometers south of the anchorage.

Lamotte-Picquet opened fire from ten thousand meters at 0619 as she emerged from behind Koh Klum. One minute later she launched three torpedoes toward silhouettes in the anchorage that were just becoming visible. At 0630 three explosions marked by geysers two hundred meters tall signified the arrival of her torpedoes. Although the French cruiser subsequently claimed to have hit a torpedo boat, and then a coast defense ship, (the *Sri Ayudhaya*) none of this salvo actually found a target. It is likely the detonations came as the torpedoes exploded in shallow waters.

Lamotte-Picquet continued to engage *Chonburi* and *Songkla* with her main and secondary batteries until 0635 when Koh Bidang fouled the range. Meanwhile, the western and central divisions closed the anchorage and met in Slukpet Bay. Between 0635 and 0650 they bombarded the torpedo boats at ranges down to three thousand meters. The French report that *Chonburi* and *Songkla* returned fire until they capsized, still at anchor. One of the boats exploded and the column of smoke rose high into the sky. Casaulties were heavy.

While the battle , *Dhonburi* was sailing south to the sound of guns (her diesels permitted her to get under way rapidly) while *Nhong Sarai* and *Theiw Uthok* withdrew north.

---

[4] The 3-inch gun's maximum range was approximately ten-thousand meters so when the Thai ships opened fire the enemy ships would have been at the limit of their range.

At 0638 *Lamotte-Picquet* spotted *Dhonburi* heading southeast, ten thousand meters to the north,and trained her turrets on this new target. *Dhonburi* replied with paired salvoes from her powerful guns. Although she enjoyed a one meter draft advantage over the French cruiser, the shallow waters still constricted her movements. She began describing tight circles as the French light cruiser continued to head run east at seventeen knots, the range periodically fouled by Koh Hai Si, which has a peak 285 meters high, and a small archipelago to the east of this island. At 0656, with the waters shoaling and her propellers churning mud, *Lamotte-Picquet* came about to the west southwest.

Between 0700 and 0715 *Lamotte-Picquet* ran southwest as Dhonburi continued southeast. The two ships swapped salvoes as openings between the intervening islands permitted. As they came in and out of view each ship had to reacquire its target. This condition affected *Dhonburi*'s accuracy more than *Lamotte-Picquet*'s as the French ship enjoyed twice as many barrels and a higher rate of fire. Then a 155-mm shell struck *Dhonburi*'s bridge and killed Captain Promwiraphan and several senior officers. Another struck the ship's engine room and damaged the steering gear. Meanwhile, the rest of the French flotilla, operating as one formation from about 0650, sailed southeast out of Slukpet Bay. By 0715 they were north of Koh Bidang and had *Dhonburi* under fire. As *Lamotte-Picquet* looped south of Koh Bidang, *Dhonburi* shifted her fire to this group and at 0720 landed a salvo a hundred meters from *Amiral Charner*.

Around 0730 the French sloops and gunboats turned south as *Lamotte-Picquet*, having circled Koh Bidang, passed them heading northeast at twenty-seven knots. Between 0735 and 0745 the range between *Dhonburi* and *Lamotte-Picquet* closed from twelve thousand to seventy-five hundred meters Moreover, *Lamotte- Picquet* ran clear of the intervening islands. With a clear line of fire, she hit *Dhonburi* several more times, knocking the Thai ship's aft turret out of action and igniting fires. *Dhonburi*, risking the shallow water, turned northwest, trying to open range. Several of her salvos fell within fifty meters of the French cruiser, but her fire was starting to slacken. The crew was operating the forward turret manually and aiming it by the ship's movements. Fires were burning out of control and *Dhonburi* was listing to starboard. At 0748 *Lamotte-Picquet* came about to the southwest and range opened rapidly as *Dhonburi* continued northwest. Two minutes later she fired another salvo of three torpedoes at an estimated distance of fifteen thousand meters. The lookouts could not observe the results because *Dhonburi* disappeared from view behind an island at 0802 and, given the extreme range, the torpedoes would not have arrived until 0803. In the event, all missed.

Figure 6. *Dhonburi*'s foreward turret and superstructure on the gounds of the Royal Thai Naval Academy.

AFTERMATH

Lamotte-Picquet ceased fire at 0802 and rejoined her flotilla southwest of Koh Kra shortly before 0840. Berenger, concerned about the threat posed by the Royal Thai Air Force, immediately set course for Saigon. The Thais had assigned two wings, each comprised of a fighter squadron and a reconnaissance squadron to the area, the first based at Nakorn Nayok (71st Fighter and 44th Reconnaissance) and the later at Chanthaburi (72nd Fighter and 32nd Reconnaissance). When the Thai air force received news of the action they reacted swiftly. Three Curtiss Hawk III biwing fighters from the 71st Squadron took off and flew toward the battle zone. They came upon the burning *Dhonburi* first and one attacked, hitting her with a 50-kg bomb that caused three additional deaths and some flooding. Realizing the mistake, the flight leader, Flying Officer Prasong Kunadilok, then led his force toward their proper target, attacking *Lamotte-Picquet* at 0848. He claimed he hit the cruiser with a 250-kg bomb, but it failed to explode. The French state that the first two bombs missed by a few meters while the rest fell further away. A second flight of Two Vought V93S "Corsair" light bombers of the 32nd Reconnaissance Squadron attacked at approximately 0900 without results.

After the French had withdrawn south, the Thai transport *Chang* arrived and took *Dhonburi* under tow and helped fight her fires. Despite this assistance, *Dhonburi* capsized that afternoon in shoal water between Koh Chang and the mainland near Laem Ngop, about two kilometers from shore. She was later raised and towed to Bangkok for repairs, but even so was never truly seaworthy again. She subsequently served as a torpedo boat depot ship. Today portions of her superstructure survive at the Royal Thai Naval Academy.

Lamotte-Picquet expended 454 rounds of 155-mm and 379 of 7-5mm (117 against the two air attacks). Her fire was effective, but the French claim that forty 155-mm rounds hit their targets is unlikely given the ranges at which the action was fought and the problems of intermittent target acquisition. In addition *Dumont d'Urville* fired 255 rounds of 138-mm, *Charner* 769, *Tahure* 85 and *Marne* contributed 54 rounds of 100-mm. *Dhonburi* fired about 100 8-inch rounds. The RTN torpedo boats were anchored and never raised enough steam to get underway; their participation in the battle was limited and ineffective before the weight of French fire overwhelmed them. The RTN suffered eighty-three deaths in this action, fifteen on *Dhonburi* and the balance on the torpedo boats. The French deny that their ships suffered any damage although Thai eyewitnesses claimed that at least one 8-inch shell struck *Lamotte-Picquet*. In view of the cruiser's subsequent movements, it is unlikely that she was seriously damaged.

The common version of Koh Chang, based upon French accounts, depicts an overwhelming French victory. "On January 17 the Thai Navy was virtually eliminated in the Koh-Chang estuary Cambodia."[5] It doubles the size of the RTN force placing the First Squadron's *Sri Ayudhaya* and *Trad* among the combatants and states that both were sunk (although later refloated). Moreover, this narrative maintains that: "without doubt, the fleet had brought the French better terms than they might otherwise have gotten in the subsequent peace negotiations."[6]

---

[5] Brown, *Warship Losses*, 41. He lists Thai losses as the Coast Defence Ships "*Domburi*" and "*Ahidea*" and the torpedo boats *Chonbun*, *Songkla* and *Trat*.

[6] Koburger, *Cyrano Fleet*, 55.

Tactically, the battle was certainly a French victory, but did it affect the naval balance of power? The RTN did not doubt that their Third Squadron had been surprised and defeated in detail by a superior force. However their ability to project power in the region was still considerable. By 20 January the RTN had collected the First and Second Squadrons at Sattahip, a force consisting of one coast defense ship, one armored gunboat, five torpedo boats and two large sloops. This fleet remained in being for the balance of hostilities and even as late as 31 January was poised to shell French positions along the Cambodian coast. The French navy, meanwhile, had made its play; its ships had expended considerable ammunition and torpedoes, all irreplaceable at least in the short term. *Lamotte-Picquet*, whether she was damaged by 8-inch fire or not, did sustain minor damage from near misses and the blast of her own guns, and it had been five and a half years since her last refit. She arrived in Saigon on 18 January and did not put to sea again until 23 February when she sailed up to Cam Ranh. The war ended as it had begun, with the RTN in control of the coastal waters off Cambodia.

Shortly after the battle Japan stepped in to mediate. The French victory at Koh Chang may have motivated the Japanese intervention, but it was more likely impelled by Thai success in the ground war. A resurgent Thailand was more dangerous to Japan than the status quo. On 28 January a ceasefire went into effect and on the 31st representatives of Vichy and the Kingdom of Thailand signed a preliminary accord aboard the Japanese light cruiser *Natori* at Saigon. On 7 February negotiations for the final settlement commenced in Tokyo and, finally, on 9 May the parties signed the final treaty. Under this treaty, Thailand regained the Laotian areas of Lao Sayaboury and west-bank Champassak and the Cambodian provinces of Battambang and Siem Reap. In return they paid an indemnity to France. Neither the French Far Eastern squadron nor the Royal Thai Navy played a significant role in the world war that followed.

Figure 7. *Dhonburi*'s foreward turret and superstructure on the gounds of the
Royal Thai Naval Academy. (source unknown)

CHAPTER 2. ATTACK AND SINK! THE ITALIAN VICTORY OFF BASTIA HARBOR: 9 SEPTEMBER 1943

In 1943 the war arrived on Italy's doorstep. In May the last of her African forces surrendered following a fifteen-hundred-mile retreat from Egypt to Tunisia. In July Anglo-American armies overran Sicily and were poised to invade the mainland. Yet, Italy was hardly defeated. Although its air force had been reduced to about a hundred modern fighters and perhaps a thousand older types, the navy retained six battleships, nine cruisers, eighty destroyers and escorts and many smaller vessels.[7] There were eighty divisions under arms, seven more than Italy went to war with thirty-nine months before. The trouble was that except for eighteen divisions, her army was deployed outside the Peninsula or consisted of low quality coastal divisions and units in reconstruction or training. Moreover, a "realization that the situation held no hope had spread among the Italian people. The growing loss of prestige had undermined the self-confidence of the nation. The numerous humiliations imposed by the German ally had increased the weariness of war."[8]

On 25 July the King of Italy, Victor Emmanuel III, ordered Benito Mussolini arrested, following a no-confidence vote by the Italian Fascist Grand Council. He formed a new government the next day under Field Marshal Pietro Badoglio. Badoglio proclaimed that the war would go on even as his government opened tentative negotiations with the Allies. But mutual mistrust, unwarranted assumptions and perhaps bad faith clouded the process and contributed to the disaster that followed. Instead of American paratroopers landing in Rome, German panzers rolled through the streets of the Eternal City. Instead of a front line overlooking the Po River valley in the north, most of Italy became a war zone, or suffered a prolonged and brutal occupation.

---

[7] Dear, *The Oxford Companion to World War II*, 596. Gardiner; *All the World's Fighting Ships*, 280-317.

[8] Von Senger und Etterlin, *Neither Fear Nor Hope*, 152.

Representatives of General Dwight Eisenhower and Badoglio signed the armistice document on 3 September, the day that British forces crossed the Straits of Messina and landed at Reggio. The two parties were to simultaneously proclaim the armistice, but Eisenhower agreed to a delay so the Italians could prepare for the German reaction and could receive the main Allied landing. However, fear of the Germans, who were pouring divisions into Italy, reluctance to accept responsibility for the nation's defeat, and mixed loyalties caused the King and Badoglio to have second thoughts.

General Maxwell Taylor, deputy-commander of the 82nd Paratroop Division, arrived in Rome on the night of 7 September, ostensibly to inspect the airfields at which his division would soon be landing. But the top commanders were unavailable to meet with him and their underlings told him Italy was not ready, was too weak, the armistice must be delayed. Taylor insisted on seeing Badoglio. Badoglio, who had been asleep, received the American general in pajamas and told him that he wanted the armistice announcement delayed. Taylor had him put it in writing to Eisenhower. The next day Eisenhower curtly telegrammed Badoglio that he would make the announcement, as agreed, "and that if I did so without simultaneous action on his part Italy would have no friend left in the war."[9] At 1830 hours on 8 September Eisenhower went on United Nations radio and announced:

"The Italian Government has surrendered its armed forces unconditionally ... Hostilities between the armed forces of the United Nations and those of Italy terminate at once. All Italians who now act to help eject the German aggressor from Italian soil will have the assistance and the support of the United Nations."

Overtaken by events, Marshal Badoglio reluctantly went on Radio Rome an hour and a quarter later and proclaimed:

"The Italian Government ... has requested an armistice from General Eisenhower ... This request has been granted. The Italian forces will therefore cease all acts of hostility against the Anglo-American forces wherever

---

[9] Eisenhower, *Crusade in Europe,* 186.

they may be met. They will, however, oppose attack from any other quarter."[10]

The result was tragic. At 0500 hours the next morning Badoglio and the King fled their capital, making no arrangements for its defense. The Army command reacted with confusion and did not clearly order resistance against the Germans as expected by the Allies. One solider remembered: "There was a flood of orders, but each one was different ... resist the Germans; don't fire on the Germans; don't let the Germans disarm you; kill the Germans; lay down your weapons; don't give up your weapons."[11] In most cases the result was "a passive acceptance of being disarmed."[12]

Sailors aboard two warships moored at Bastia, on the Italio-German occupied island of Corsica, listened to Badoglio announce the armistice with wonder, shock and disbelief. Few realized they would soon be engaged in bitter combat against their old ally. The Battle of Bastia Harbor which followed early the next morning is a largely forgotten episode that stands out against modern Italy's most ignominious moment; it demonstrates, in spite of the collapse of Italy's army and government, how Italian sailors and soldiers performed given strong leadership and a clear mandate to fight.

The torpedo boats *Aliseo* and *Ardito* departed Genoa the evening of 7 September 1943. These were a type of warship about the size of an American destroyer-escort and they served much the same function. They were escorting the new fast motor ship *Humanitas* (7,980 gross registered tons) on her maiden voyage to La Maddalena, Sardania. *Humanitas* was armed with twelve machine guns and two larger anti-aircraft guns and was loaded with three thousand tons of ammunition, vehicles and fuel. The torpedo boats displaced 1,830 tons full load and were armed with two 100-mm 47-calibre guns and ten (*Aliseo*) or twelve (*Ardito*) 20-mm 65-calibre antiaircraft weapons. They were rated at twenty-four knots, but could do twenty-six in a pinch. Like *Humanitas*, both were new ships, being launched in 1942 and entering service in 1943.

---

[10] Italian Surrender Documents. http://www.geocities.com/iturks/html/documents_11.html

[11] Agarossi, *A Nation Collapses*, 105.

[12] *Ibid.*, 104.

Figure 8. Map of the campaign area and tracks of the naval action at Bastia.

Figure 9. The Italian torpedo boat *Aliseo*, a modern escort of the *Ciclone* class commissioned in early 1942. She displaced 1,160 tons standard and carried two single 100-mm/47 guns, ten 20-mm/65 and four 450-mm torpedo tubes. The *Ciclones* could make twenty-five knots and were a rugged, well regarded design. (Erminio Bagnasco collection)

Allied air superiority forced the Italians to sail by night, staging from port to port. At first light on the morning of 8 September the small convoy arrived at Bastia and moored along the mole in the order of *Humanitas*, *Ardito* and finally *Aliseo*, which, as flagship, was the last one in. They joined the Italian motor-torpedo boat *MAS 543*, the Italian freighter, *Sassari* and two German submarine chasers or *Unterseebootsjager* of the 22nd Flotilla. Later that day a group of five MFP (*Marinefahrprähme*) armed barges arrived from Elba.

Corsica and Sardinia were front-line targets and garrisoned accordingly. On Corsica the Italian Army deployed its VII corps. Commanded by Major General Giovanni Magli, it consisted of two infantry and two coastal divisions along with miscellaneous battalions.[13] They shared the island with the 16th SS Brigade (Assault Brigade "Reichsführer"). On Sardinia two Italian army corps formed the bulk of the garrison, but it also included the German 90th Panzergrenadier Division and the 183rd and 184th regiments of the Italian (but pro-German) Nembo paratroop division. *General der Panzertruppe* Fridolin von Senger und Etterlin commanded the

---

[13] Pignato and Cappellano, "L'Esercitoitaliano dall'armistizio al trattato di pace," 45.

German force. He had arrived only on 7 September having previously served in Sicily as German liaison officer to the Italian 6th Army.

Badoglio's armistice instructions were simple, but the reality was not. Italy had fought alongside Germany for over three years. Many officers and men supported the alliance and its war aims. Italian forces were mingled with the Germans throughout the Mediterranean and Balkans; this was especially true in Bastia where German ships shared port with Italian ships and German troops manned defenses alongside Italian troops. Mario Cardea, the radio operator aboard *Aliseo,* remembered hearing the news:

"Our ships passed a normal morning. In the afternoon men were granted shore leave. Towards 1800 hours the news that the armistice had occurred hit us like lighting.... We were astounded. As soon as they learned the news, the crew on shore spontaneously returned back aboard, recalled by their deep sense of duty, attachment to their ship and to their Captain."[14]

One German soldier detached from the SS brigade had different memories. "The town was full of drunken Corsicans and Italians, some of them armed and looking for Vichy French soldiers to kill. In the town square the people started to sing the *Marseillaise* along with the *Internationale*, the flags of the Allies along with many communist banners were hoisted. Anti-German graffiti appeared on every wall. The situation was tenuous."[15]

Germany had anticipated Italy's separate peace. Badoglio had hardly finished his broadcast before German forces sprang into action. That night the 16th SS Brigade seized the town of Bonifacio on Corsica's southern tip. At noon the next day German forces assaulted Italian coastal artillery positions on the Maddalena Islands, offshore from Sardinia's principal northern port of La Maddalena. Naval forces attacked Portoferraio, the chief city of Elba and the Tuscan port of Piombino. The Germans were attempting to secure the chain of harbors necessary to withdraw the their troops from the islands and the most important link in that chain was the harbor of Bastia. About five hours after Badoglio's broadcast, German ships in the port received the coded message: "Prepare Harvest."

---

[14] Cardea, "La Brillante Azione Della Torpediniera Aliseo," 2.
[15] http://www.reenactor.net/kb/articles/schonhuber.htm

Figure 10. German MFPs entering Bastia harbor prior to the Italian armistice. The port was protected by a long breakwater seen on the left of the photo. (copyright unknown)

It was a half-hour before midnight. At that moment, *Aliseo* had just slipped her moorings and was making for the narrow passage between the two jetties that enclosed Bastia's outer harbor. Commander Carlo Fecia di Cossato, captain of *Aliseo*, was following his standing orders; *Humanitas* was expected in La Maddalena, a hundred miles to the south before light the next day.

The captain of *UJ 2203* observed the convoy's preparations to follow *Aliseo*. He radioed: "Bring in the Harvest." A siren began to wail.

Aliseo had just cleared the port when the rapid, popping sound of heavy machineguns crackled across the water. *Ardito* was under concentrated fire from *UJ 2203* and *UJ 2219*, as well as German-manned guns aboard *Humanitas*. The attack was so intense it drove the torpedo boat back against the mole, slaughtering 70 men from her crew of 180. Then German sailors from the sub-chasers and the barges stormed the stricken warship. A passenger aboard *Humanitas* remembered:

> "At 2330 the silence of the night was disrupted by a loud whistle which was their signal to attack. This woke me. Simultaneously all the ships anchored in port were attacked. The lookouts, one by one, were stabbed or killed with hand grenades and for an hour we stood in danger of suffering the same fate. All of the guns aboard were concentrated on us and we had no choice but to throw ourselves on the ground .... In the stern hold a fire broke out ... Some of the motor vehicles fell prey to the flames, their tanks as well as a lot of gasoline drums exploded into the air. The fire also threatened the other holds which were loaded with explosives .... On my hands and knees I crawled towards the ladder that was crowded with terrified, panicked soldiers."[16]

Meanwhile *Aliseo* cruised off-shore, her guns manned and ready to open fire. Commander Fecia di Cossato was an experienced veteran, Italy's leading submarine ace (now serving in surface forces for health reasons) and the holder of two silver medals for valor as well as an Iron Cross, second class and the Knight's Cross. He was fearless and cautious as only a successful submarine skipper can be. Although tempted to return to the rescue of his sister ship, Fecia di Cossato radioed the port commander, Admiral Gaetano Gonzaga, for instructions. At 0148 hours Gonzaga ordered him to remain outside the harbor rather than face the German batteries. This he did, sailing in a north-south pattern twelve nautical miles offshore. In town the battle subsided as Italian seamen were taken prisoner and confined aboard two of the barges and German sailors moved in to occupy the city.

At 0459 Gonzaga radioed that Bastia had fallen and ordered Fecia di Cossato to bombard the German ships in the harbor. However, he decided to wait until dawn to avoid damaging any friendly units. This was a good decision as the situation remained fluid. Italian Blackshirt infantry rallied outside the city and, supported by armored cars, they counterattacked. A nearby Luftwaffe flak unit of five hundred men armed with powerful 88-mm guns remained neutral. The Italian reinforcements drove the German sailors back to their boats. Refusing a demand to surrender, they released their harvest of prisoners and began getting underway.

---

[16] Lovatto, "In Corsica doppo l'8 de settembre, Il Diario di Giovanni Milanetti."

At 0700 hours *Aliseo* received further instructions: Bastia was back in friendly hands. The German ships were fleeing. "Attack and sink!" As he read this signal, Fecia di Cossato had just come about to the north and was about thirteen nautical miles southeast of the harbor. His emotions may have been somewhat ambiguous. He had served most of the war in France, operating out of German bases. Just six months before, Germany had awarded him the Knight's Cross, up until that time something only five other Italians had received. Yet, whatever ambiguity there was in his emotions, there was no ambiguity in his response. He ordered *Aliseo* to head northwest and rang up full speed.

A light fog hung over the shore. From this mist lookouts aboard *Aliseo* saw the enemy vessels emerge one-by-one from the narrow mouth of the port and turn to the north hugging the coast.

The German flotilla was far superior to *Aliseo* in every respect except speed. It consisted of two submarine chasers: *UJ 2203*, ex-*Austral*, a former fishing vessel and French Navy aircraft transport, 63.4 meters long, grossing 2,234 tons, and *UJ 2219*, formerly the Belgium motor yacht *Insuma*, 35 meters long and built in 1938. Following the sub-chasers came *F 366, 387, 459, 612* and *623*. These motorized barges displaced 220 tons full load and were 47 meters in length. Finally, there was a 43-ton Luftwaffe motorboat *FL B 412*. The two sub-chasers had 88-mm guns while the barges were all armed with one 75-mm and either a 37-mm or 20-mm gun. The motorboat had a single 20-mm. *Aliseo*'s only advantage was speed; *UJ 2203* could steam at eleven knots and the barges at 10.5 knots compared to her twenty-six knots.

Figure 11. *Aliseo* at Bastia making a hard turn to starboard leaving a German UJ boat burning in her wake. (Erminio Bagnasco collection)

Aliseo closed range rapidly as *UJ 2203* opened fire followed by other German units as they bore. *Aliseo* maneuvered to avoid the fall of shot, withholding her reply until 0706 when she was less than eight thousand meters from the German column. For the next twenty-five minutes she ran north, roughly parallel to the German line, maintaining range and firing rapidly until 0730 when an 88-mm shell hit *Aliseo* in her engine room. Emitting a great cloud of steam she drifted to a halt. But her crew rapidly repaired the damage and plugged the holes to minimize flooding; she was able to get underway and continue the action before the Germans could escape.

Aliseo overhauled the German column by 0815 and, turning west, closed the enemy from the northeast. The shorter range improved her accuracy as 100-mm shells struck *UJ 2203* and several of the barges. At 0820 *UJ 2203* exploded, killing nine men and sending an enormous column of smoke into the air. *Aliseo* shifted her fire to *UJ 2219* and ten minutes later she too exploded and sank.

Figure 12. *UJ 2203* exploding offshore north of Bastia taken from *Aliseo*. (copyright unknown)

Meanwhile, the column of motor barges, maintaining an intense fire, began to break up as each vessel fled on its own. Anti-aircraft shells riddled *Aliseo*'s fire control director forcing her guns to continue under local control. But with the ranges nearly point blank, this hardly mattered. One crewmember recalled: "The Captain continued to maneuver to shorten the range. We locked onto a group of three motor barges. We were so close we were able to duel with machineguns. We were hit profusely with 20-mm projectiles, but they failed to inflict serious damage."[17]

By 0835 *Aliseo* had sunk three barges. At 0840 she engaged two more that were loaded with ammunition. These boats were also being shelled by Italian shore batteries at Marina de Pietro and by the Italian corvette, *Cormorano*, which had just arrived. Caught three ways, they ran themselves ashore. The Luftwaffe motorboat was also sunk.

---

[17] Cardena, "La Brillante Azione Della Torpediniera Aliseo," 3.

Figure 13. UJ indicates *unterseebootsjager* or submarine hunter. The Germans pressed into service a wide range of vessels to serve as escorts and submarine hunters. *UJ 2219*, an ex-Belgium yacht was smaller than most displacing only 280 grt. *UJ 2203* was an ex-French fishing trawler that displaced 1,188 grt. (copyright unknown)

Captain Fecia di Cossato ceased fire at 0845, his ammunition nearly all gone. Between 1000 and 1050 hours *Aliseo* rescued twenty-five German survivors, ten severely wounded. She then made course for La Specia until ordered instead to Portoferraio, reaching that port at 1758 hours that afternoon.

The battle had lasted one hour and thirty-nine minutes. Despite the sustained intensity of enemy fire, *Aliseo* only suffered light damage and no fatalities. In contrast, 160 German sailors lost their lives.

In its first surface action against the Kriegsmarine, the Regia Marina won a complete victory. The tactical consequences, at least in terms of the Corsica campaign, were significant. The senior German naval officer captured during the fighting, a Lieutenant Rohwer, claimed he did not know anything about an order to attack—whatever had happened was the fault of the naval group commander who, unfortunately, had died and thus could not be held accountable for his strange conduct.

Figure 14. Commander Carlo Fecia di Cossato during the 9 September engagement. (Erminio Bagnasco collection)

During the afternoon of 9 September Italian light forces—torpedo boats *Aliseo, Ardimentoso, Fortunale, Ariete, Indomito, Calliope* and *Animoso*, corvettes, gunboats and motor torpedo boats—rendezvoused at Portoferraio. The captains debated what course they should follow, but finally satisfied they would not be required to lower their flags or otherwise be subjected to dishonor, the flotilla set sail for the Allied control port of Palermo on the 10th.

This fleet surprised the Americans when it appeared off the Sicilian port without notice on the 11th. The port commander had just received a copy of Admiral Cunningham's signal that the Italian fleet lay at anchor under the guns of the fortress of Malta. He felt like replying: "Be pleased to inform Their Lordships that Palmero lies under the guns of an Italian fleet!"[18]

That same day *Humanitas*, her damage repaired, finally got underway for La Maddalena. But she didn't make it far. The Dutch submarine *Dolfijn* was lurking off Bastia. She observed *Humanitas'* departure, but not

---

[18] Morison, Sicily-Salero-Anzio, 244.

the black flag which Italian ships were supposed to fly to acknowledge their acceptance of the armistice. Moreover, *Dolfijn's* captain believed the harbor was German occupied. For these reasons he attacked *Humanitas* at 1548 hours, firing four torpedoes and blowing off the freighter's stern. *Humanitas* lasted for several hours before being attacked again, this time by eight German aircraft. She was finally beached, a total loss.

On Corsica the strategic implications of the Italian victory proved shorter-lived.

The Germans began transferring the 90th Panzergrenadier Division from Sardinia to Corsica on 9 September via their newly captured base of La Maddalena. Meanwhile, the 16th SS Brigade secured Bonifacio on Corsica. The Italian VII Corps did little to interfere, concentrating instead in the island's mountainous interior, except for some battalions occupying Bastia, which the army needed to maintain communications with Italy.

Bastia was also key to General von Senger if he wanted to evacuate his artillery and vehicles, but he had to delay a confrontation with the VII Corps until he had more troops at hand. Finally, on the 12th he told General Magli to order the evacuation of the city or face attack. That same day the SS brigade, advancing north along the coast highway, captured Casamozza twenty kilometers south of the port. The Italians, in turn, imprisoned the Germans remaining in Bastia, including elements of the Luftwaffe flak unit, whose neutrality in the battle of three days earlier had been a factor in the Italian victory.

The next morning the 16th SS attacked north, but the advance proceeded slowly. The Italians blew up a highway bridge behind the German front lines and kept the approach roads under artillery fire. Finally, a German thrust conducted under the cover of dark brought the SS troops into the city as the defenders withdrew to the north and west.

After that the rest of the story can be quickly told.

On 15 September a French battalion landed at Ajaccio to help the Italian garrison and the local marquis hurry the Germans on their way. On 20 September the Italian and Germans forces exchanged 800 German prisoners for 3,000 Italians. The Germans evacuated Bonifacio that night.

During their withdrawal, the Germans destroyed every airfield and bridge on Corsica's east coast; they wrecked the harbor installations at

Bonifacio and Porto Vecchio. Von Senger departed aboard the last German ship to evacuate Corsica on 3 October 1943. Italian Bersaglieri entered the port just three hours later. More than 6,200 German and pro-German Italians, 3,200 vehicles and 5,000 tons of supplies escaped over 60 miles of open water to continue the fight in Italy. At its peak the evacuation involved 15 steamers and 120 smaller craft. It was a poor ending to a naval campaign that had begun so well. Italian admirals had proposed their force of five destroyers and twelve torpedo boats be deployed to complete the job *Aliseo* had started and cut the sea lanes between Bastia and Tuscany. Instead, *Aliseo* and her sisters swung at anchor in Malta, hostages to an uncertain peace.

PIOMBINO 11 SEPTEMBER 1943

The night of 8/9 September Italian forces defeated another German surprise attack at Piombino, the mainland terminus of Germany's evacuation route from Sardinia and Corsica.

Six MFP armed motor barges loaded with four hundred troops and crew arrived at Piombino that day, joining four MFPs already in port. After Marshall Badoglio announced the armistice that evening, the port commander, Commander Amedeo Capuano contacted the Germans and secured their promise to sail at dawn the next morning. Instead, German sailors disembarked after dark, disarmed Italian patrols, and occupied a coastal battery near the harbor. After the Germans ignored several demands to withdraw, Commander Capuano ordered a machine gun unit to fire on their boats. Then a shore battery of 3-in guns located north of the harbor joined in. In fifteen minutes, the Italians sank two barges and severely damaged a third. Outgunned and surprised by the violence of the Italian reaction, the German sailors released their prisoners and retreated to their boats, claiming, as they had in Bastia, that the whole affair was a case of mistaken orders.

Figure 15. *MFP769* – The MFPs were versatile ocean-going barges that could carry up to 200 tons of supplies. Five tried to escape Bastia when Italian troops retook the town on the morning of 9 September. *Aliseo* supported at a distance by *Cormorano* sank one outright and forced four to scuttl. (courtesy of Peter Kreuzer)

On 9 September the surviving barges withdrew but they did not go far. The situation remained tense as desertions began to unravel some Italian army units. At 0200 on 10 September two torpedo boats escorting a stea-mer appeared offshore. These were *TA9* and *TA11*, small destroyer equiva-lents armed with a pair of 100-mm guns but even at that the heaviest Ger-man naval units in the western Mediterranean. They tried to trick their way into the harbor, claiming to be Italian. When that ruse failed, they re-quested permission to refuel. After protracted negotiations, the local army commander overruled Commander Capuano and agreed that they could enter port if they departed immediately after taking on supplies. At 0800 the German warships moored so their guns covered both the northern and southern portions of the harbor.

At 1140 *TA11* turned its guns on four Italian VAS boats (*Vedetta Anti Sommergibile* , or anti-submarine launches) entering the port and forced them to moor alongside, imprisoning their crews. At noon, the Germans had finished refueling, but they refused to leave. Hampered by desertions, the army considered ceding the port, but Commander Capuano refused stating he would require orders from naval command before he could undertake such an action.

Throughout the day, German intentions became increasingly clear: eight barges, three anti-submarine launches and one motor minesweeper entered port. Citizens from the city and workers from the dockside factories gathered guns and occupied some of the army's old defensive positions. That night German patrols began infiltrating out from the harbor. In an attempt to observe these movements, the Italians ignited a rocket flare at 2045 and the German captain, thinking this was the signal for an Italian attack, ordered his forces to open fire. The Italians did not reply until the torpedo boats began bombarding the batteries, then the engagement became general. Italian soldiers and sailors, reinforced by citizens, repulsed the German attacks. *TA9* got underway, exchanging salvos with a 3-in shore battery, but she withdrew after suffering several damaging hits. *TA11* fired from her mooring at the south mole. An Italian shell struck one of the captured Italian VAS boat tied alongside her igniting a fire. Oil floating on the water turned this into a conflagration that quickly enveloped *TA11*. By 0300 hours the Germans had everywhere been defeated.

The day of the 11th the Italians mopped up and took prisoners. The burned out hulk of *TA11* broke free of her mooring and sank. Wrecks of the MFPs and lighter boats littered the harbor. Only the motor minesweeper escaped. However, as in Bastia, a local victory could not change the strategic situation. On 12 September reconnaissance units of the 24th Panzer Division and the 305th Infantry Division entered Piombino and the city definitively passed into German hands.

CHAPTER 3. THE ROYAL NAVY'S REVENGE: THE BATTLE OF PENANG STRAIT, 16 MAY 1945

In the 1930s British military planners designated Singapore the Empire's most strategic point, short of the home island itself. They regarded Japan as a major threat and expected to establish a balanced fleet at Singapore's great naval base to protect India to the west, Australia to the south and Malaya to the north. But in 1941 when the need arose, the fleet was committed. The navy had suffered heavy losses in more than two years of solitary warfare against Germany and Italy and could dispatch to the Far East only two capital ships to join a patchwork squadron of elderly cruisers and destroyers. Then, just two days after hostilities commenced, Japanese bombers caught *Prince of Wales* and *Repulse* as they hunted a Japanese invasion force and sank them both.

In January, February and March 1942 large British and Commonwealth warships fought five battles against the Imperial Japanese Navy off Endau, in the Java Sea, at Sunda Strait, off Borneo and in the Indian Ocean south of Java. In all five the Japanese routed their former mentors (the British provided training and built warships for the young Japanese navy up through the First World War and in many respects Japan based its fleet on the British model) sinking a sloop, five destroyers, and two cruisers at the cost of a few ships moderately damaged. Although Great Britain reinforced the Indian Ocean with old battleships and a few modern carriers the Japanese drove this fleet all the way to the east coast of Africa causing its commander, Vice Admiral James Somerville, hero of Gibraltar's Force H and many Malta convoys, to inform the Admiralty: "Enemy has complete command of Bay of Bengal... Our present naval forces and land-based air forces are quite inadequate to dispute this command. The Battlefleet is slow, out-gunned and of short endurance."[19] The Royal Navy continued to avoid battle with the Japanese for more than two years. By the middle of 1944, however, the situation had changed. With Italy's defeat Great Britain could finally base a strong fleet at Ceylon and, at long last, strike back.

---

[19] Simpson, *Somerville Papers*, 403.

Figure 16. Japanese heavy cruiser launched in 1929. She was a powerful ship armed with a main battery of ten 8-inch guns, eight 5-inch dual purpose guns and sixteen torpedo tubes. She displaced 13,380 tons, and had about twice as much protection as American cruisers with similar armament. *Haguro* participated in the East Indies, Solomon, Midway, Central Pacific and Philippine campaigns. She is pictured here under air attack at Rabaul on 2 November 1943. (Naval Historical Center)

As British strength waxed, Japanese strength waned. The heavy cruiser *Haguro* joined the 10th Area Fleet at Singapore on February 25, 1945. This once mighty force mustered a pair of cruisers and a destroyer plus assorted mine vessels, submarine chasers and patrol craft. *Haguro*'s busy career mirrored the wartime fortunes of the Japanese navy. She sank a destroyer and two cruisers at the Battle of the Java Sea and off Borneo in February and March 1942. She screened the carriers at Coral Sea and helped capture the Alaskan islands of Attu and Kiska in June 1942. She fought in the Solomon campaigns and in the cruiser duel of Empress August Bay in 1943. *Haguro* survived the Battle of the Philippine Sea and sailed in the armada that squandered an overwhelming advantage against

American escort carriers in the action off Samar, the decisive engagement in the Battle of Leyte Gulf that occurred in October 1944.

Figure 17. A *Nachi*-class cruiser, probably *Haguro* under air attack during the battle of the Sibuyan Sea, October 1944. (US Navy)

By March 1945 Japan still occupied vast territories, but they were shrinking fast. After a long campaign that had more to do with Imperial pride and the lack of a coherent strategy than with military necessity, the British finally arrived at the banks of the Irrawaddy River in Burma and began infiltrating down the Burmese coast via small amphibious landings. In February 1945 the East Indies Fleet, based at Trincomalee, Ceylon started sending destroyer patrols (from bravado the destroyer sailors called them "club runs") into the Bay of Bengal to harass the enemy.

Figure 18. Captain Manley L. Power, commander of the 26th Destroyer Flotilla on the bridge of *Saumarez* during the 19 March action in Stewart Sound. (from John Winton, *Sink the Haguro*)

The 26th Destroyer Flotilla under Captain Manley L. Power with *Saumarez*, *Volage*, and *Rapid* departed Trincomalee on 14 March on the third of these sweeps. It began uneventfully. They bombarded a train on Sumatra, fruitlessly scoured the coast of the Nicobars and looked into an empty Port Blair on the Andamans. It might have been a training exercise. On March 19, 1945 Power led his ships to Stewart Sound between North and Middle Andaman Islands. *Saumarez* negotiated a narrow, bent passage and discovered a junk moored alongside a pier. The destroyer's gunners began peppering this meager target, and then the rumble of heavy gunfire erupted from behind. A hidden 6.1-inch shore battery had surprised *Rapid* guarding the sound's seaward entrance. Five shells smashed into the destroyer damaging the boiler rooms and leaving her dead in the water. When she returned *Saumarez* found *Rapid* dead in the water, a large fire raging amidships and plumes of steam and smoke boiling up from her funnels.[20] Power's flagship passed a tow line while *Volage* stood off, trying to distract the battery by furiously returning fire with her 4.7-inch guns. In this she succeeded too well; three shells struck *Volage* and disabled her steering. The British destroyers finally managed to escape. *Rapid* lost eleven men killed and twenty-one wounded while *Volage* had three killed and eight wounded. Despite the heavy butcher's bill the British were

---

[20] Winton, *Haguro*, 32.

lucky. The battery's 123-pound shells could have easily sunk one or more of the unarmored destroyers.

Figure 19. The destroyer *Rapid* at Stewart Sound, 19 March 1945. She is stopped, hit in both boiler rooms by 6.1-inch shells from a Japanese shore battery. A smoke float drifts to starboard. (from John Winton, *Sink the Haguro*)

On March 25th Vice-Admiral East Indies Fleet gave the 26th Flotilla, now including *Saumarez*, *Virago*, *Vigilant*, and *Volage*, another chance. They headed east and at 1030 the next morning found the submarine chasers *Ch-34* and *Ch-63* escorting a convoy of two small freighters, *Rishio Maru* (1,500 tons) and *Teshio Maru* (400 tons) carrying rice, reinforcements, and women for the Andaman garrison. This time Power handled his ships too cautiously. Sailing in line ahead, *Saumarez* opened fire at 1059 targeting *Teshio Maru* from 14,000 yards, beyond the range of the single 3-inch/40 gun that armed each of the submarine chasers. The other ships joined in as they bore.

The sea was calm and the air clear. The destroyers fired rapidly, their 4.7-inch guns capable of shooting twelve 62 pound rounds a minute. After one pass which left the enemy unharmed, *Virago* closed to four thousand yards. Four torpedoes whooshed into the water running toward *Rishio Maru*, but every one missed. *Volage* launched four more and these missed as well. At 1129, with the untouched convoy fleeing southwest, Power called in a pair of patrolling Royal Air Force B-24 Liberators. The leading aircraft attacked at mast-level. It sank *Teshio Maru* with a well placed stick of bombs, but got caught in the blast and went spinning into the sea.

Figure 20. Captain Manley Power's flagship *Saumarez* leads a column of destroyers. This was taken during her Arctic service in the. (from E. March *British Destroyers*)

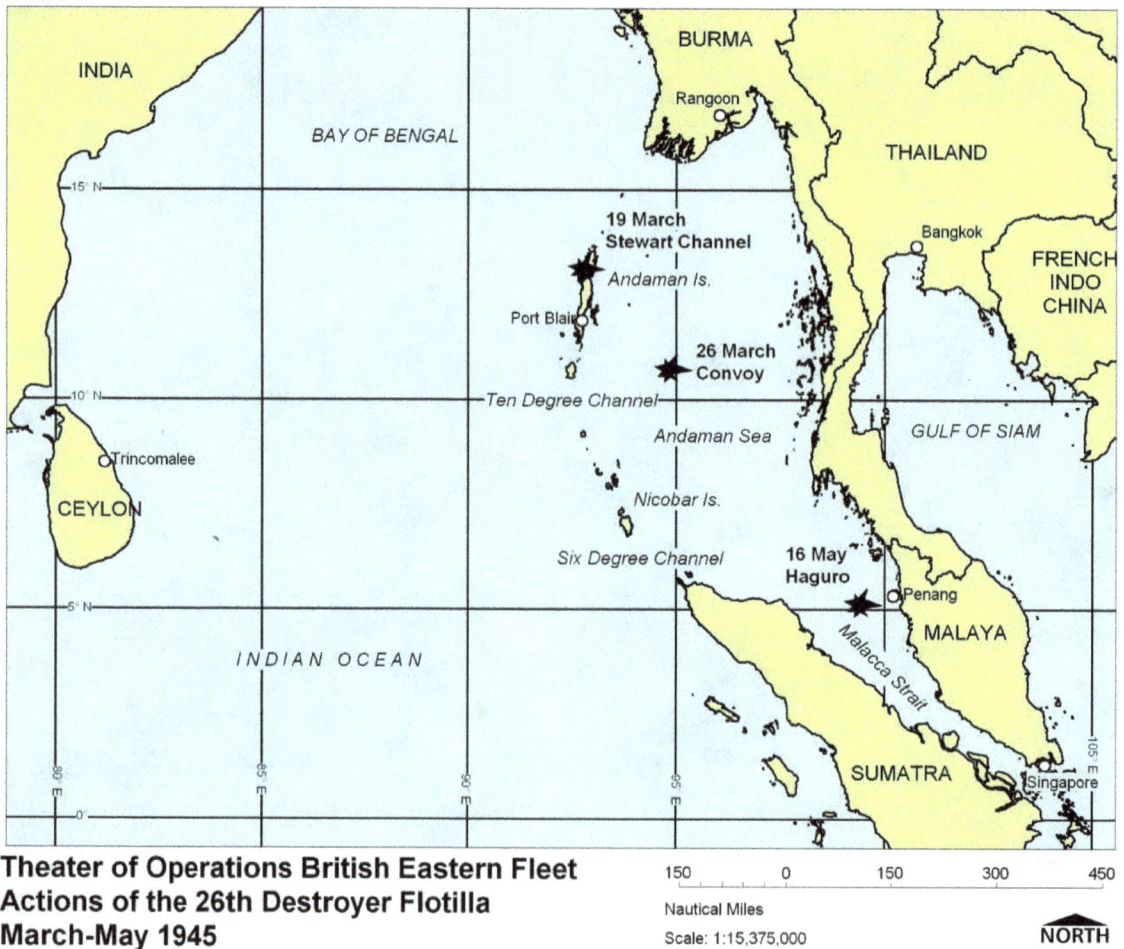

**Theater of Operations British Eastern Fleet
Actions of the 26th Destroyer Flotilla
March-May 1945**

Figure 21. Overview map of British Eastern Fleet Actions of the 26th Destroyer
   Flotilla March – May 1945. (V.P. O'Hara)

Power's destroyers had worked around to the south of the convoy during the bombing run and at 11:50 they renewed their attack. The subchasers fled as the destroyers finally crippled *Rishio Maru*. *Volage* finished her
off while *Saumarez* rescued the B-24 crew and *Vigilant* and *Virago* pursued the subchasers. *Volage*'s captain wrote: "I had not realized how easy
it was to get rid of some 900 rounds (of ammunition) in a short space of
time."[21]

---

[21] *Ibid.*, 38.

By 12:30 p.m. *Vigilant* and *Virago* had the subchasers under fire from long range. The Japanese skippers fought their small ships (one-quarter the size of their British opponents and capable, at sixteen knots, of only half their speed) with determination and skill. They maneuvered smartly and successfully chased salvos, vacating a patch of water just before enemy shells arrived. *Vigilant* finally closed and, foregoing half measures, emptied all eight of her torpedoes tubes. One ran true and exploded against *Ch-63*. Her captain reported: "It was as though the whole of the forepart was blown out of the water and folded backwards over the bridge."[22] The sub chaser sank in just seconds, but her sister managed to exact a small revenge. A member of *Vigilant*'s crew recalled: "After training our tubes fore and aft a 4" shell from the other frigate hit our Bofors ammunition locker and went right through ... three partitions of steel to explode in the catwalk over the after tubes ... (and) a hail of small fire rattled along our decks."[23]

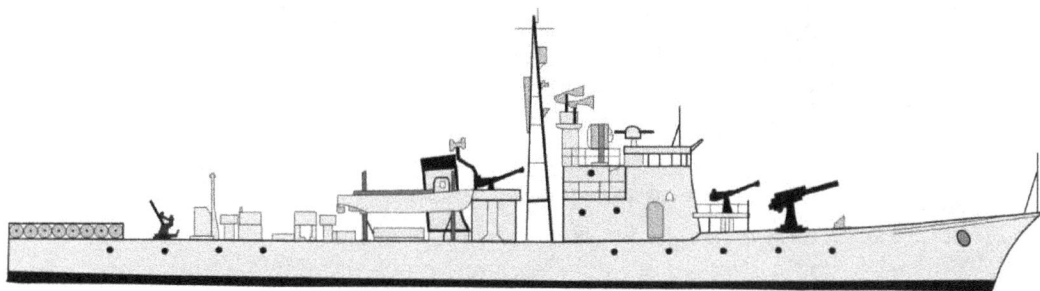

Figure 22. Japanese submarine chaser *Ch-63*. She displaced 460 tons and carried one 76-mm/40 gun. (V. P. O'Hara)

As *Ch-34* fought back. *Vigilant* and *Virago* closed to Bofors range, having nearly exhausted their supply of 4.7-inch ammunition. Finally, at 4:30 p.m., seven and a half hours after the battle began, little *Ch-34* succumbed, her guns still firing even as she sank. *Vigilant* returned to the site where the steamers sank and rescued some survivors, including one Filipina woman who could speak English, but left many more to drown. A crewman remembered "someone on the forecastle shouting up to the Captain, calling him a bastard for leaving women in the sea."[24] In total Power's four ships expended 3,160 4.7-inch rounds and 18 torpedoes. The

---

[22] *Ibid.*

[23] Hough, HMS *Vigilant.*

[24] Ibid.

British official history dryly noted that "the Admiralty, not surprisingly, described the action as 'unsatisfactory.' "[25]

The 26th Flotilla was making a name for itself, but so far it was nothing to be proud of.

Figure 23. Wreckage from the convoy attack of 26 March when two small Japanese escorts fended off four British destroyers for over seven hours before succumbing. The two transports were carrying civilians as well as military supplies. A woman can be seen resting on the debris. (from John Winton, *Sink the Haguro)*

On April 23, 1945 the Japanese army evacuated Rangoon, Burma's capital just before Indian troops landed below the city. Destroyers sweeping the bay in advance of the assault claimed sinking nine small vessels carrying a thousand Japanese troops, but Captain Power's ships missed this action. They screened *Queen Elizabeth* and *Richelieu* when these battleships bombarded Port Blair on 6 May. Their big guns revenged *Rapid* leaving massive craters where the Japanese battery at Steward Sound had been. The fleet returned to Trincomalee on 9 May, in time to celebrate the end of the war against Germany.

---

[25] Roskill, *War at Sea,* 316.

Figure 24. The composition of the 26th Flotilla varied according to availability but generally included ships of the S-V (war emergency) class. *Viriago* is pictured here. Originally fitted for Arctic service the V class displaced 1,808 tons; their armament included four single 4.7-inch guns and eight 21-inch torpedo tubes. (from John Winton, *Sink the Haguro*)

The Andaman Islands guarded the sea lanes to Malaya, but the club runs had isolated them and by May 1945 the Japanese garrison faced starvation. On 9 May the 10th Area Fleet sent two of its last three major operational units, *Haguro* and the destroyer *Kamikaze,* along with two submarine chasers from Singapore to bring in supplies and evacuate excess troops. Signals intelligence gave the plan away. British submarines in the Malacca Straits unsuccessfully attacked the Japanese and Task Force 61 under Vice Admiral H. T. C. Walker, consisting of *Queen Elizabeth, Richelieu,* three cruisers, four escort carriers and eight destroyers, sailed from Trincomalee to intercept.[26] In turn, Japanese reconnaissance aircraft spotted Walker's ships and the commander, Rear Admiral Shintaro Hashimoto wisely turned back on the night of 11 May.

In light of the Andaman garrison's desperate situation, Hashimoto sailed again on 15 May. Walker, anticipating this move, had stayed at sea hiding south of Six Degree Channel. At 0217 hours on 15 May he released the 26th Flotilla, now with *Saumarez, Verulam, Venus, Virago,* and *Vigilant* to sweep the seas around Sumatra's northern tip. Power craved inde-

---

[26] The British submarine *Subtle* reported *Haguro* was painted pink. This has led to speculation the submarine's commander mistook the color in the light or that *Haguro* was painted a shade used by the British navy called Mountbatten pink from stocks captured in Singapore

pendent action, but one officer recalled: "I had not been keen on going out again, least of all against a cruiser when the war was supposed to be over."[27] Power continued at twenty-seven knots steaming deep into enemy waters until 1041. Then, because Walker lacked hard intelligence about *Haguro*'s whereabouts, the Admiral recalled Power's flotilla. However, Power had just received an aircraft's sighting report that sounded promising, so he delayed obeying Walker's order. Then at 1150, while searching for a ditched aircraft, a British airplane finally spotted *Haguro*, escorted by the old destroyer *Kamikaze*. Due to mechanical difficulties and crowded flight decks, Walker required six hours to put a three plane strike into the air. *Haguro* had long since come about and was steaming hard for Singapore. The trio of Grumman Avengers conducted the longest British carrier strike of the war and the Fleet Air Arm's first dive bombing attack on a cruiser since 1940, but their mission failed to inflict any damage. Meanwhile, Walker sent a battleship and a heavy cruiser forward to support the 26th Flotilla, but only Power's ships could catch *Haguro*.

Figure 25. HMS *Venus.* (from John Winton, *Sink the Haguro)*

As darkness fell, the five destroyers sailed south into the Strait of Malacca eighty-five miles southeast of *Haguro*'s reported position and between her and her base. In a letter to his wife Power set the stage: "It was a pitch dark night, with dense black clouds and occasional tropical rain, lit fitfully by vivid lightning. A proper stage setting for a rather desperate venture."[28] At 2245 hours the unusual atmospheric conditions enabled *Venus* to establish radar contact with the enemy at the incredible range of

---

[27] Winton, *Haguro*, 77.

[28] Thompson, *War at Sea*, 251.

thirty-four miles. As Hashimoto's force closed to twenty-six miles Power swung his flotilla to the north in line abreast and reduced speed to twenty knots.

At 0003 hours, with the range down to twenty-eight thousand yards, the flotilla reversed course to the south and reduced speed to twelve knots to keep a tell-tale wake from showing in the incandescent sea. Power strung his ships in a rough crescent from northwest though south to east. If *Haguro* obligingly entered the crescent, the destroyers would torpedo her from all sides. However, at 0100 on 16 May *Haguro*'s lookouts reported suspicious shapes and her commander, Captain Kaju Sugiura ordered his helmsman to zigzag at twenty knots, maintaining a southeasterly heading. Even still, all seemed well from the British point of view. At 0050 Power ordered his flotilla to come about and head toward the enemy. *Haguro* loomed dead ahead of *Saumarez*, range twelve thousand yards and closing rapidly. Then four minutes later Japanese lookouts shouted an alarm. Sugiura reversed course to starboard and began working up to thirty knots heading northwest. Power, facing the prospect of a sprung trap and a stern chase, also range up full speed.

At 0105 *Haguro* came back around to the southeast. She now lay fine on *Saumarez*'s bow, range six thousand yards and closing at thirty yards a second. The British ships held fire to keep their locations hidden. Then *Kamikaze* suddenly appeared just three thousand yards off and *Saumarez* had no choice; her forward guns erupted with flashes of flame as she swerved hard to starboard to avoid crashing into the Japanese ship. *Saumarez* passed behind *Kamikaze* and her 40-mm Bofors raked the surprised enemy's deck killing twenty-seven men and injuring fourteen. Power's flagship then twisted to port closing the cruiser as starshell erupted overhead. With a target finally in view *Haguro* fired a full eight-gun broadside.[29] A crewman aboard *Saumarez* recalled:

> "All this time I had been conscious that the familiar crack of our 4.7s and the thump-thump-thump of my own guns were being blotted out by a gigantic hammering storm of tremendous noise, drowning all speech and sense. *Haguro* was firing on us, point-blank ..."[30]

---

[29] Turret No. 2 had been knocked out at the battle of Leyte Gulf by a 1,000-pound bomb and never repaired.

[30] Winston, *War at Sea*, 376.

In the space of a few minutes 277-pound shells sheered off *Saumarez*'s funnel and gashed her forecastle.

> "The sea was spouting with shell splashes all round us. We were drenched to the skin with near misses and water streaming everywhere as we closed the range. Our guns still firing rapid broadsides into the destroyer and hell's delight going on with enemy salvos screaming over the ship."[31]

But it was a fifty-one pound 5-inch shell that did the most harm, hitting the boiler room and severing the main steam-pipe. As a large fire erupted amidships *Saumarez*—two men killed and three badly burned—lost speed. Nonetheless, the starboard screw still revolved at full power. The ship skewed around broad on the cruiser's beam. At 0113 the first of eight torpedoes leapt from her tubes, the others following at timed intervals while *Saumarez*'s black gang worked frantically to restore power. Sugiura thought he had disabled one destroyer and was training his heavy guns on *Verulam* when, at 0114, *Verulam* began launching six "fish" from fine on the cruiser's bow, range two thousand yards. A pair of torpedoes from these salvos, each packing 810 pounds of Torpex, exploded near No 1 and No. 3 turrets. Making smoke, *Saumarez* escaped northwest to sort out her damage as *Verulam* headed east. *Haguro*'s speed fell and flooding quickly produced a list to port. *Kamikaze* fell in behind the cruiser, but Hashimoto ordered her to Penang and she succeeded in escaping into the night.

Three destroyers still maneuvered to attack and Sugiura ordered abrupt alterations in course trying to disrupt their aim. Star shells and flares exploded overhead; the roar of guns mingled with the rumble of thunder. The torpedo concussions cut *Haguro*'s electric power and her turrets couldn't train. After a time the two aft turrets began to fire again, but under local control and without the accuracy of their first salvos. At 0125 *Venus* closed to twenty-five hundred yards and sent six torpedoes toward *Haguro*'s starboard side. Two minutes *Virago* launched seven torpedoes toward the same side. A rocket showed her enemy "almost stopped with a huge list of some 40 degrees to port."[32] At least one torpedo from these salvos struck *Haguro* in the engine room. Sugiura ordered smoke, but, with the cruiser losing way, it hung in the air giving scant concealment.

---

[31] Thompson, *War at Sea*, 251.

[32] Winston, *Haguro*, 136.

Shortly thereafter a salvo of 4.7-inch shells exploded on the cruiser's bridge, slaughtering Hashimoto and most of his officers and mortally wounding Sugiura in the stomach.

Finally, at 0151 *Vigilant*, her torpedo solutions fouled up to this point by her sister ships, closed to eighteen hundred yards and fired eight torpedoes. In March she pegged a subchaser from further away, but this time she missed. At 0202 *Venus* fired her last two torpedoes from twelve hundred yards. "We opened up with Bofors and their pink tracers were very spectacular as they curved towards the now stopped cruiser with its deck awash and after part covered with billowing thick black smoke."[33] Altogether the 26th Flotilla launched thirty-seven torpedoes. They claimed nine hits and at least three torpedoes found their target. This was enough. The veteran warship sank bow first at 0232 forty-five miles southwest of Penang. Power's ships unsuccessfully tried to fish a prisoner or two out of the water and then made off at speed. The next afternoon *Kamikaze* rescued 320 survivors from *Haguro*'s complement of twelve hundred men.

In the larger scheme of the war, even in terms of British plans to reconquer their lost colony of Malaya, Captain Power's victory had little significance. Rather, its importance was psychological. "It was a heartening success for the East Indies fleet at last to sink a major Japanese warship."[34] The British navy had returned to the waters where they suffered their greatest defeat in modern times. The navy redeemed itself in an old fashioned gun and torpedo action, sinking a major warship that had triumphed over British forces in similar actions three years before. The battleships and cruisers didn't get a chance because the 26th Destroyer Flotilla led the way.

---

[33] *Ibid*, 142.

[34] Roskill, *White Ensign*, 437.

Figure 26. The "Action Information Centre" of HMS *Saumarez*. (from John Winton, *Sink the Haguro)*

CHAPTER 4. DEFIANT UNTIL THE END: THE NAVAL CAMPAIGN IN THE CHANNEL ISLANDS

The Channel Islands were the only British territory occupied by Germany in World War II. The liberation of this archipelago off Normandy's Cherbourg Peninsula might have seemed mandatory as a matter of prestige, but when the Allies conquered Normandy they chose instead to blockade and isolate the German garrison. This strategy led to a miniature and hard-fought naval war within a war around the islands, far behind the front lines, that lasted nearly a year until the destruction and surrender of the Nazi regime in May 1945.

The German navy had five destroyers, six torpedo boats, thirty-eight motor torpedo-boats (S-boats) and 319 minesweepers and patrol vessels (from the large *M* classes down to motor-minesweepers and converted fishing trawlers) deployed in French waters in June 1944.[35] The handy and versatile *M* class minesweepers formed the backbone of this fleet. These 775 ton vessels could sail at seventeen knots and were armed with a 4.1-inch/45 gun, a 37-mm and seven 20-mm machine guns. They were "extremely well designed and suited to a variety of tasks, including escort, anti-submarine warfare, anti-aircraft cover and minelaying. Russian naval intelligence referred to them as small *M*-type destroyers!"[36]

In the two weeks following D-Day, Germany's offensive warships—the destroyers, torpedo boats, and S-boats—fought a series of futile battles. On 8 June the British, Canadian, and Polish 10th Destroyer Flotilla intercepted the German 8th Destroyer Flotilla in transit from Brest to the battle zone. In a long and confused night action the Allies sank *Z32* and *ZH1* and badly damaged *Z24*. German S-boats raided the invasion fleets nightly and fired a prodigious number of torpedoes. They sank twelve ships and damaged another six.[37] Although these attacks hardly dented the stream of Allied supplies flowing to France, they provoked a hard strike

---

[35] Tarrant, *Last Year*, 41.

[36] Gardiner, Fighting Ships 1922-1946, 245.

[37] Tent, *E Boat Alert*, 144.

against the German navy. On the evening of June 14 the Royal Air Force's Bomber Command struck Le Havre and obliterated Germany's naval strength in the Channel east of the Allied beachhead. More than twelve hundred tons of bombs sank the torpedo boats *Falke*, *Jaguar*, and *Möwe*, fourteen S-boats and thirty-nine other craft, and damaged most of the survivors.

Figure 27. A row of M-class minesweepers. This photo gives a good view of their 4.1-inch guns. (courtesy of Przemyslaw Federowicz)

In the Gulf of St. Malo and around the Channel Islands, however, the German navy was still a factor. The veteran 24th Minesweeper Flotilla (large *M* class ships *M343*, *M412*, *M424*, *M432*, *M442*, *M452*, and *M475*) led by *Fregattenkapitän* Fritz Breithaupt had been sweeping mines, escorting convoys and asserting Germany's control over the coastal waters since 1940. The 46th Minesweeper Flotilla under the young *Kapitänleutnant* Armin Zimmermann, made up of converted trawlers numbered sequentially *M4600* through *M4628*, and the 2nd Patrol Boat (*vorpostenboote*) Flotilla, made up of converted trawlers numbered *V201* through *V216*, supported the 24th. These ships maintained the lifeline between the Channel Islands and the mainland. Although the Allies anticipated a German withdrawal, in fact, Axis convoys sailed nearly every night, weather permitting, rushing supplies to the islands and evacuating construction workers and political prisoners.

Figure 28. German trawlers at sea. The V-boats of the 2nd and the minesweepers of the 46th Flotilla were generally fishing trawlers pressed into military service. These coal burning vessels were especially valuable as they did not draw upon the Kriegsmarine's limited supplies of fuel oil. (courtesy of Przemyslaw Federowicz)

After their victory on the night of 8 June the ships of the 10th Destroyer Flotilla patrolled across the Channel into the Gulf of St. Malo to suppress this traffic. On the night of 13 June the Polish destroyer *Piorun* (Commander Tadeusz Gorazdowski, Senior Officer) and the British destroyer *Ashanti* were sailing from Île de Batz to Jersey, looking for enemy destroyers, minesweepers or submarines. The wind was blowing from the southwest at twenty knots, lifting short, crested waves in the shallow waters of the gulf. There was a heavy overcast and visibility was only four to six thousand yards. At sea that night six minesweepers of the 24th Flotilla along with assorted V-boats were escorting a small convoy from St. Malo to St. Peter's Port in Guernsey.

Figure 29. *Piorun*'s men cleaning her 4.7-inch guns. (courtesy of Przemyslaw Federowicz)

At 0025 hours on the 14th *Piorun*'s radar operator picked up four pips that seemed to be ships headed north at fifteen knots. The destroyers turned to investigate. At 0037 at a range of 2,300 yards their 4-inch guns fired star shell. The drifting flares illuminated a line of three large minesweepers. The destroyers immediately opened fire and their 4.7-inch shells hit the lead German ship hard. But the minesweepers turned toward the larger enemy ships and fought back: "their returning fire was both vigorous and, as always with the Germans, accurate."[38] One 4.1-inch shell exploded near *Piorun*'s No. 4 gun and detonated ammunition, wounding four men and igniting a small fire. A second round damaged the destroyer's aft 20-mm gun mounting and wounded two more men. At 0048 the Polish destroyer responded by firing her full load of five torpedoes; one ran true and exploded against *M343*'s bow, leaving the sweeper stopped and gravely damaged.

---

[38] Peszke, *Poland's Navy*, 157.

Figure 30. A German minesweeper crew posing for the camera. (courtesy of Przemyslaw Federowicz)

Figure 31. German M-class boats conducting a minesweeping operation in the English Channel. (courtesy of Przemyslaw Federowicz)

The destroyers were steaming north, northeast drawing close to Jersey. At 0057 there was the roar of heavy guns, and star shells from the 8.66-inch guns at Battery "Roon" on Jersey's southwestern promontory flashed overhead. Faced with this threat the Allied ships made a high-speed turn. During this evolution *Piorun* damaged her gyrocompass and at 0113 she fell back, letting *Ashanti* take the lead. As they steamed southwest two more German ships emerged from the darkness two miles to the south and two others about the same distance to the northeast. The Allied ships swung to the northeast and at 0132 they commenced fire at these new targets. As ranges closed to only a thousand yards machineguns joined in. The Germans fired back and small-caliber shells punctured *Piorun*'s quarterdeck. This action was over by 0155 as the German ships vanished in the smoke and dark. But only five minutes later *Piorun* picked up more radar contacts. Once again the Allied destroyers turned in pursuit. *Ashanti* fired star shell (the Polish destroyer had used up all of hers) illuminating minesweepers about four thousand yards east. The two groups exchanged fire and the Allies claimed they set three enemy ships on fire. *Ashanti* finished off her star shells but the destroyers kept firing using radar to acquire targets.

At 0228 Battery Roon intervened once again and two minutes later, magazines nearly empty, the destroyers turned for home. The number of shells fired indicated the intensity of the action. *Piorun* expended 679 rounds of 4.7-inch, 104 of 4-inch, 100 star shells and 1,260 40-mm shells. A witness on Jersey remembered: "watchers from the south coast reported that the sky was lit like daylight by the numerous star shells during the action."[39] The Allied destroyers claimed three minesweepers sunk and one more severely damaged. In fact, the toll was much less. *M343* sank at 0240 hours; *M412* was moderately damaged and had four men wounded. *M422*, *M432*, *M442*, and *M452*, all suffered light damage. In fast-moving night actions it was hard to really know what really happened and claims of damaged inflicted were often exaggerated.

Two nights later Lieutenant Commander J. H. R. Kirkpatrick's Canadian 65th MTB Flotilla was in action. *MTB 726*, *MTB 745*, *MTB 727*, and *MTB 748*, all 115-ft type "D" motor torpedo boats armed with a six-

---

[39] Le Sauteur, *Jersey Under the Swastika,* 12-13.

pounder gun and four torpedo tubes, crossed the Channel on a routine patrol. Having reached the southern end of their beat, they were cruising north along the Cherbourg Peninsula near Cap de Flamanville when radar indicated ships steering south, southeast about three thousands yards to the west. This proved to be a convoy of two *M* class minesweepers, three trawlers and two merchantmen. The Canadians tried a stealthy approach, but when the Germans challenged they rushed to attack. *MTB727* fired two torpedoes from fifteen hundred yards, followed by *MTB748* from twelve hundred. The Germans illuminated with star shell and laid down a heavy defensive fire. The Canadians closed to point blank range and passed up the side of the convoy blasting it with their Hotchkiss six-pounders; then they circled around and ran pass the enemy formation once more before retiring north. Because there were no explosions they believed their torpedo had missed, but in fact they hit *M133*. The survivors towed the heavily damaged minesweeper to St. Hélier and later to St. Malo where she was scuttled on 6 August.

That same night the Islanders saw the flash of gunfire on the west shore of the Cherbourg Peninsula. To defenders and residents both an invasion seemed eminent, but on 19 June the weather imposed a temporary truce. An unseasonable gale blew up and huge seas swept the Channel, keeping surface forces, particularly coastal craft sheltering in port.

After the weather moderated, the Germans began running convoys again and the Allies continued trying to stop them. On June 22 the 65th Flotilla's *MTB 748*, *MTB 727*, *MTB 745*, and *MTB 743,* along with four British MTBs of the 52nd Flotilla, conducted a joint operation off Jersey. A German patrol drove away the 52nd, but the 65th found a convoy near St. Hélier consisting of an S-boat, a minesweeper, a pair of armed trawlers and the merchant ship *Hydra.* The Canadian MTBs began their high speed dash from four thousand yards out, but the escort illuminated and opened fire. A shell exploded in *MTB 745*'s engine room. She drifted to a stop while *MTB 748* wrapped her in a smoke screen. *MTB 727* and *MTB 743* pressed on, their six-pounders blazing. Then *MTB 748* caught up and her shells ignited a large fire aboard *Hydra.* *Hydra* eventually sank, but *MTB 745* made it home at six knots, the best speed she could manage in her damaged condition. It was a long journey.

On the night of 26 June the "D" class MTBs of the 52nd Flotilla had better luck off Jersey when, in poor visibility, they snuck up on ships of the 46th Minesweeper Flotilla. The MTBs opened fire from four hundred yards and then circled and launched torpedoes. One struck and sank *M4620*. German return fire was heavy, but only one man of the 52nd lost his life and just two were wounded.

The battle between the 24th Flotilla and *Ashanti* and *Piroun* demonstrated that the *M* class minesweepers could stand up to destroyers, but only at great risk. It might seem the converted fishing trawlers were completely outmatched by large, modern destroyers, but a small action fought the night after *M4620* sank illustrated the danger of night engagements, even for destroyers fighting trawlers. *Eskimo* and *Huron* had the duty that night. They intercepted *M4611* and two patrol boats, *V213* and *V203:* all formerly fishing trawlers, smaller, slower and less capable boats than the six M class ships their flotilla mates had sparred with two weeks before.

Figure 32. The Tribal class destroyer HMS *Eskimo*. A shell form *V213* disabled this veteran of the battles of Narvik and Brittany (www.navyphotos.co.uk.)

The destroyers shelled *M4611* and set her afire and, after maneuvering around and investigating a false contact, returned to finish off the two patrol boats. *V213*, meanwhile was emitting a dense screen of smoke. *Eskimo* entered the smoke, but the 282-ton trawler, whose heaviest weapon was an 88-mm gun, struck first and hit *Eskimo* twice. An 88-mm shell exploded in the British destroyer's No. 1 boiler room and a 37-mm round pierced the main steam line in No. 3 boiler room. The powerful warship, ten times the size of her enemy, lost steering and could only steam in circles at six knots. She eventually made it back to Plymouth while the pesky *V213* escaped to St. Hélier.

Several days later on the night of July 3 several of *V213*'s flotilla mates fell prey to Kirkpatrick's 65th Flotilla. *MTB 748*, *MTB 743*, *MTB 735*, and *MTB 736* lay waiting with lights extinguished and engines quietly idling north of Ile de Chausey. Their target was a convoy sailing from St. Hélier for St. Malo including the ex-tug *Minotaure* carrying 468 Russian laborers and civilians. She was led by *V210,* a fishing trawler constructed in 1934 and armed with an 88-mm and several 20-mm guns, followed by *V209*, *M4622*, and *V208* at the convoy's rear. Kirkpatrick quietly led his boats to a position in front of the Germans and at 0132 hours on July 4, when the Germans were just eight miles north of their destination, the Canadian boats announced their presence with flares. Engines roared to life as one pair of boats attacked the head of the convoy from about three thousand yards with torpedoes and the others struck the rear. Their barrage was unusually deadly. A torpedo detonated in *V210*'s engine room. She broke in two and quickly sank. *Minotaure* took two torpedoes in her bow and another near her rudder, but fortunately for the hundred crammed aboard, she somehow stayed afloat. A fourth torpedo slammed into *V208* and she followed her flotilla mate to the bottom. The Canadians closed in and fired at the German ships as they raced pass. The *V209* and *M4622* returned fire. The action was over in just four minutes. Twenty men from the two patrol boats died, but the survivors rescued forty-five others. *MTB 748* was holed and limped home down by the bow carrying five wounded men. In port her crew counted fourteen shell holes. *MTB 743* suffered slight damage and had one wounded.[40]

On the night of 7 July *Huron* and *Tartar* had the offshore patrol. They intercepted elements of the 46th Minesweeper Flotilla and sank *M4605* and *M4601*. The rest of the German force ran for port where shallowing water and coastal batteries forced the destroyers to turn away. The balance of the month was relatively quiet. Poor weather kept the coastal craft in

---

[40] http://www.divernet.com/wrecks/wtour500403.htm.

port. After the heavy attrition, which had seen the Germans lose two large minesweepers, six armed trawlers and a supply ship off the Channel Islands in the four weeks following D-Day, they only lost *V209* in the next four weeks in an Allied air raid on St. Peter's Port on 24 July.

During this period of relative calm at sea, the land campaign intensified. Cherbourg fell on 27 June. On 25 July the Americans broke the stalemate in their decisive attack around St. Lô and the 4th and 6th armored divisions raced into Brittany. An air raid on 4 August caught *M424* in St. Malo Roads and damaged her beyond repair. On the night of 6 August the surviving units of the 24th Minesweeper Flotilla—*M412, M432, M442,* and *M452*—evacuated St. Malo in the face of the advancing American army. An Allied force consisting of two destroyers supporting motor torpedo-boats intercepted Breithaupt's ships off Jersey. The Channel Islanders heard heavy gunfire from this engagement, but the Allies could not prevent the remnants of the 24th from fighting through to St. Hélier. *V215* and *M133* were too damaged to sail and had to be scuttled at St. Malo. The port held out until 17 August assisted by raiding parties from the Channel Islands equipped for anti-tank fighting. The navy would sneak these troops one night and bring them out (usually) the next. They also evacuated hundreds of wounded men.

With the German navy squeezed off the mainland, the Allies proceeded to quarantine the Channel Islands. The battles in western Normandy and Brittany were both American operations and, after 2 August, the containment of the German fleet became the responsibility of the United States Navy. To accomplish this task the Americans teamed destroyer escorts with PT Squadron 30 (PTs *450-461*), and PT Squadron 34 (PTs *498-509*) operating out of Cherbourg and began to patrol the waters around the islands every night. Their British liaison, Lieutenant Commander Peter Scott remembered: "Our routine was to meet in Cherbourg at four in the afternoon with the plans for the night; then set off at five in the P.T. boats for a rendezvous with the destroyers among the islands. At daybreak we returned to Cherbourg and, after a belated breakfast, planned the operations for the next night."[41]

---

[41] Scott, *Narrow Seas*, 207.

On the night of 8 August the American destroyer escort *Maloy* accompanied *PT-503*, *PT-500*, *PT-507*, *PT-508*, and *PT-509* to the waters west of Jersey. At 0530 hours on the morning of 9 August *Maloy*'s radar picked up contacts off St. Hélier which proved to be six trawlers of the 46th. In calm, foggy conditions the PT boats closed in. Two boats launched torpedoes by radar and missed. Then *Maloy* sent *PT-508* and *PT-509* roaring in at forty knots. They each fired a torpedo from four hundred yards, missed again and circled to make a gunfire attack. But *PT-509* entered a rent in the fog as she turned away and came under heavy fire. Aflame, she turned back and rammed one of the minesweepers. The German crew "were blazing away with small arms and tossing hand grenades down on the PT."[42] They managed to crowbar her off; after that she sank and only one badly wounded man survived to be taken prisoner. *PT-503* and *PT-507*, searching for their missing mate, engaged a minesweeper in St. Hélier roadstead, but were driven off with two killed.

On 11 August the American destroyer escort *Borum* supporting *PT-500* and *PT-502* attacked two ships of the 24th Minesweeper Flotilla off La Corbiere on the southwest coast of Jersey. The American PT boats fired a pair of torpedoes each, but failed to inflict any damage on the German vessels. Heavy gunfire sent the Americans on their way after wounding three men aboard *PT-502* and one on *PT-500*.

On the night of 13 August the British destroyers *Onslaught* and *Saumarez* with *Borum*, *PT-505*, *PT-498* and two British MTBs engaged *M412*, *M432*, *M442*, *M452*, and a merchant vessel off St. Peter Port. The minesweepers inflicted slight damage and some casualties on the destroyers and suffered light damage in return. *Borum* vectored the two American PT boats in toward the German flotilla. The Germans illuminated when the small boats were five thousand yards distant, but the PTs pressed on and launched two torpedoes each from fifteen-hundred yards. *PT-505* laid smoke as they turned away under heavy fire. The torpedoes all missed, but the PTs retired undamaged.

On 19 August there was an engagement between Allied forces and a convoy from Guernsey escorted by the 24th Flotilla which lasted past dawn. The Allies heavily damaged *M432* and then harassed the German

---

[42] Bulkley, *Close Quarters*, 360.

force "all the way from Grosnez (in northeastern Jersey) until it got into St. Aubin's Bay, and close enough inshore for the coast batteries to take a hand." The minesweepers "came into harbour fastened abreast of each other and towed by a tug, their antics suggesting that the steering of one was deranged, whilst increasing smoke as they approached the pier clearly suggested that one of them was on fire."[43]

After this action a period of relative calm ensued as the American army liberated Brittany. With the 24th and 46th Flotillas keeping largely to port, the United States Navy discontinued offensive patrols. The Germans occupying the islands remained dug in and isolated as supplies began to run low. Autumn passed on to winter. Their continued resistance formed a bright spot in Hitler's briefings. To assure it continued he promoted *Vizeadmiral* Friedrich Hüffmeier, former captain of *Scharnhorst* and a fervent Nazi, to fortress commander in February 1945. Hitler preferred naval officers for these postings because, as he reasoned: "many fortresses have been given up, but no ships were ever lost without fighting to the last man."[44]

The lack of supplies and coal (the *M*-class minesweepers were all coal burners) was Hüffmeier's biggest problem and he was anxious to play some part in the war that had seemingly passed him by. By coincidence, the Allied were shipping coal to the nearby port of Granville, which had good rail connections to Paris, in their effort to keep the French capital warm during the winter of 1944/45. Some German prisoners escaped from the mainland and made their way back to Jersey and told Hüffmeier about the collier convoys and this gave him an idea. He could strike a blow at the Allies and improve his own situation as well.

Hüffmeier's first attempt to raid Granville on the night of 6 February 1945 failed due to weather and the vigilance of an American patrol craft. The Germans, however, were not discouraged and prepared a second, larger force to try again. On the night of 8 March 1945 a small fleet under *Kapitänleutnant* Carl-Friedrich Mohr (Breithaupt had died in a plane crash some weeks before) consisting of *M412*, *M432*, *M442*, *M452*, a tug, three artillery lighters, three fast launches and a pair of armed trawlers sailed

---

[43] Le Sauteur, *Jersey Under the Swastika*, 12-13.
[44] Cruickshank, 285.

from St. Hélier. That night the United States submarine chaser *PC-564* (463 tons, one 3-inch gun, one 40-mm, two 20-mm, and nineteen knots), under the command of Lieutenant Percy Sandel, USNR was on routine patrol outside of Granville Harbor. At 2244 hours on the 8th Granville tower radioed *PC-564* there were three unidentified radar contacts between Jersey and Iles Chausey. Sandel turned his ship due west and sailed to intercept just beyond Chausey. The submarine chaser's radar picked up a contact 10,200 yards to the west northwest at 2359 heading south. She closed to 3,800 yards and then fired a spread of three star shells. These revealed two targets. Sandel ordered another trio of star shell trying to better fix what he was facing. After these burst *PC-564* turned to starboard to run broadside to the enemy. Her 3-inch gun fired one round and then the breech block jammed. Mohr's minesweepers suffered no such disadvantage. "Within a matter of a few seconds, and just as we had started turning, we received a hit from a large caliber gun, in the front of the pilot-house which killed all of the personnel in the pilot-house."[45]

The American's port-side 20-mm and her 40-mm located astern opened fire, but they were quickly silenced when two more shells struck in rapid succession, one at the mast which killed or wounded the 20-mm crews and another astern that took out the 40-mm crew. German star shells were falling heavy around the American ship keeping her pinned in their harsh light. Sandel wrote: "Tracer fire became more intense at this time and as there was no organization of the crew and all the guns were out, it was decided the only thing to do was to stand by to abandon ship."[46] After stopping the engines in preparation to going over the side, Sandel changed his mind, "it appearing that there was a great deal of difficulty in letting the life rafts go and the firing having decreased in intensity, it was decided not to abandon ship."[47] However, fourteen men didn't get the word and jumped into a raft they had released over the fantail.

---

[45] Sandel, "Statement," 1.

[46] *Ibid*, 2.

[47] Sandel, "Action Report," 2.

Figure 33. American submarine chaser that fell afoul of the German 24th Minesweeper Flotilla during the Granville raid of 8 March 1945 (US Navy)

The luckless *PC-564* finally got underway, steering directly for Pierre de Herpin Light on the mainland, chased by star shell and under the impression the enemy was following. Sandel ran his ship aground at 0130 hours to seek help for his wounded men. All told the minesweepers hit the American ship four times, killing fourteen and wounding eleven. The Germans rescued the men who prematurely abandoned ship and they sat out the war's final months as prisoners.

Despite Sandel's fears of pursuit, Mohr's ships headed straight for Granville and were inside the artificial harbor by 0100 hours on the 9th. Despite the radar warning and fireworks from the naval battle, the garrison was caught by surprise. Ninety German troops stormed ashore in rubber boats as the minesweepers stood off and machined gunned the quay. The troops destroyed the port facilities and liberated sixty-seven German prisoners; they killed two U.S. Marines, six Royal Navy personnel and captured six Americans "some still clad in pajamas."[48] Everything went as planned except that *M412* grounded on a mud bank in the outer harbor. At 0300 hours Mohr gave the order to retire. With the ebbing tide, however, he was only able to tow away one collier loaded with 112 tons of coal. His men sank the others. There was no time to salvage *M412* and her crew

---

[48] Morison, *Invasion*, 308.

blew her up. Then, the German fleet returned to St. Hélier well pleased with their victory.

Eleven months after two Allied armies invaded France a large and active German force survived on the Channel Islands. The narrow and shoal-ridden waters saw a dozen naval actions ranging from hit and run motor torpedo-boat raids to full blown naval battles in a protracted campaign to neutralize this Axis stronghold. Although these battles pitted modern destroyers and heavily armed motor torpedo-boats against coal burning minesweepers and converted fishing trawlers, the Allied navies were unable to completely suppress their German enemies and they had their noses bloodied on more than occasion.

The defender's attitude and their arrogance were well demonstrated on May 8, 1945, when, after the collapse of Germany, the destroyer HMS *Bulldog* approached Guernsey to receive the German surrender. A minesweeper from the 46th, "dirty, battered ... her sides red with rust, the paint on her superstructure chipped and discolored,"[49] brought Kapitänleutnant Zimmermann out to parlay. When the British general stated he expected an immediate surrender, Zimmermann replied he would have to inform Hüffmeier. He then stated: "I am instructed to inform you that your ships must move away immediately from these shores. If they do not Admiral Hüffmeier will regard their presence as a breach of faith and a provocative act!"[16][50] There were those 12-inch guns to consider and the British destroyers stood off. They duly received the surrender the next day, but it was clear the defenders of the Channel Islands felt they had never been defeated.

---

[49] Hawkins, *Destroyer*, 322.
[50] *Ibid.*, 323.

Figure 34. A German officer is speaking with a British policeman on the occupied island of Jersey, July 1940. (from *Island in Danger*, Alan and Mary Wood)

THE CHANNEL ISLANDS AT WAR

In 1940 94,000 people inhabited the Channel Islands. Jersey, the largest at forty-five square miles had 50,000 residents; Guernsey had 42,000 people on twenty-five square miles. Six hundred people lived on Sark's three square miles while 1,400 crowded Alderney's two square miles. Tiny Herm, Jethou, and Burhou were all unpopulated. When Great Britain elected to demilitarize the islands on June 19, 1940 there was some panic as people scrambled to get out. All of Alderney left, as did 17,000 of Guernsey's people and 6,600 from Jersey. On Sark, everyone stayed. On June 30 four German transport planes landed at Guernsey's airport and the occupation became a fact.

At first, the occupation was uneventful. The Germans were anxious to learn how British civilians could best be governed while the President of Guernsey's controlling committee created a stir when he broadcast that: "there was no gun pointed at his head, nor was he reading from a typescript thrust into his hand by a German officer" but he wanted to say "the conduct of the German troops was exemplary and he was grateful for their correct and kindly attitude toward the Islanders."[51]

The honeymoon survived several small and unsuccessful commando raids. However, after Hitler invaded the Soviet Union it was clear the occupation of the Islands was no longer a test case for the conquest of England. The Führer grew worried Great Britain would attack the Channel Islands in force as a matter of honor and to relieve pressure on the Russians. This worry become a preoccupation and on 20 October 1941 Hitler declared: "The permanent fortifying of the Channel Islands to convert them into an impregnable fortress must be pressed forward at maximum speed." In 1943 a German newspaper reporter filed this report: "Hundreds of thousands of cubic meters of concrete now protect the coasts, many more will follow ... Dense minefields and mile-long anti-tank walls hermetically seal the beaches ... and form a ring of steel around these former British possessions, which lie anchored like fortresses in front of the Atlantic Wall."[52] On June 1944 work was still going on, even to the detriment of far more important mainland defenses. "The Atlantic Wall would have been

---

[51] Cruickshank, *The German Occupation*, 78.

[52] *Ibid.*, 192.

doubled in strength, so far as excavated works are concerned, had the resources devoted to the Islands been retained on the mainland."[53] Bunkers, strong-points, observation posts, underground complexes, and elaborate artillery emplacements with guns of up to 12 inches in diameter studded the islands of Jersey, Guernsey and Alderney. To occupy these works, German deployed nearly 24,000 troops of the 319th Infantry Division, Naval Artillery Battalion 604, the Luftwaffe, and service and construction units. In June 1944 11,266 troops occupied Guernsey, Jersey had 8,869, and Alderney 3,443. Even as the Allies established their first beachheads in Normandy Generals Rommel and von Rundstedt petitioned Hitler to withdraw the 319th Division, but on June 17 Hitler declared that the Channel Islands would be defended *"Bis zum Aussersten"* – "To the last."[54]

Figure 35. The Polish "J" class destroyer *Piorun.* (courtesy of Przemyslaw Federowicz)

---

[53] *Ibid.*, 188.

[54] Wood, Islands in Danger, 182.

Figure 36. *Piorun*'s captain, Commander, Tadeusz Gorazdowski receiving a decoration. (courtesy of Przemyslaw Federowicz)

Figure 37. Loading torpedoes aboard *Piorun*. A priest is apparently blessing the activity. (courtesy of Przemyslaw Federowicz)

Figure 38. German naval officers aboard HMS *Bulldog* on 9 May, 1945.
Kapitänleutnant Zimmermann is sitting to the right. There is a BBC
microphone on the desk. From (*Island in Danger*, Alan and Mary Wood)

CHAPTER 5. MYSTERY BATTLE OFF IMPERIA, 1 OCTOBER 1944

At sea the fog of war lays thick, especially at night. Imperfect perceptions, false assumptions, fatigue and other human frailties affected the outcome of nearly every nocturnal naval engagement fought during the war. Even aids like radar or powerful illuminates often confused more than they clarified. Many of the hundreds of night actions fought in Europe's narrow waters by small warships such as motor-torpedo boats and minesweepers were poorly recorded and some remain completely unknown. Engagements involving destroyer-sized units, on the other hand, numbered in the dozens and historians have identified and established the outline of nearly every one.[55] One of the very few exceptions occurred off Imperia on Italy's Ligurian coast in 1944.

This article examines a little-known night engagement between a U.S. destroyer and a German flotilla of two torpedo boats and a destroyer that occurred off Imperia in Northern Italian Riviera on 1 October 1944. This action has remained unknown because each side failed to properly identify the nature of their opponent: the Germans believed they had engaged and damaged a French light cruiser and two destroyers while the American thought they destroyed two merchant ships from a convoy of three. That it required sixty years to document the actual events of this action is of interest both as a case study in the way assumptions can determine the course of a battle and then the subsequent record, and as a historical detective story.

THE ENVIRONMENT

In one of the war's lesser known naval campaigns, the Kriegsmarine, assisted by the small navy of the *Repubblica Sociale Italiana* (RSI), conducted a tenacious struggle in the Tyrrhenian and Ligurian Seas in defense of a vigorous coastal traffic and to harass Allied naval forces from Sep-

---

[55] According to the author's tabulations, fifty surface actions involving destroyer types (but nothing larger) on each side occurred during World War II. Eighteen took place in the Mediterranean, thirteen in the English Channel, thirteen in the Pacific and six elsewhere in European waters.

tember 1943 to the end of the war.[56] German ships transported 1,500 to 2,000 tons of materials a month because supplies could be more safely carried to the front by sea than by land. As Great Britain's official historian ruefully noted: "Though the constant harassing of the German convoys by our coastal craft must have given them a good deal of trouble, the actual losses we inflicted were small in relation to the traffic carried on those routes."[57]

Initially the opposing fleets consisted mainly of armed barges, motor-torpedo and motor-gun boats, minesweepers and subchasers. The Germans, however, rushed to outfit captured Italian torpedo boats and destroyers to give their coastal flotillas more weight. These were called TA boats which stood for *Torpedoboote ausländisch* or foreign torpedo boat. Eventually these consisted of a mixed collection of ex-Italian, French, even Yugoslavian warships, and included brand new vessels as well as relics from the First World War.

The first two of these ex-foreign warships entered service in December 1943. By February 1944 the Germans had commissioned enough destroyer-types to organize the 10th Torpedo Boat Flotilla, known as the *todesflottille* or death flotilla, under *Korv. Kapt.* Wirich von Gartzen. It operated from Genoa and La Spezia laying minefields, bombarding Allied positions ashore and escorting convoys. Casualties were heavy, as the flotilla's name implied, but the shipyards of Genoa continued to refit or repair enough ships to maintain the 10th's strength. Meanwhile, Allied destroyers generally stayed south to escort convoys and, after January 1944, to guard the Anzio beachhead.

In the summer of 1944 two events radically transformed the Western Mediterranean naval situation. First, the Allies finally cracked the Italian front after an eight-month stalemate and began to roll through central Italy, capturing Rome on 4 June 1944 and reaching a line north of Pisa and

---

[56] See Tomblin. *With Utmost Spirit*; Tarrant, *Last Year of the Kriegsmarine*; Roskill. *War at Sea*; and O'Hara. *German Fleet at War* for overviews of this campaign. The RSI operated MAS boats and special attack units. The infamous Decima MAS unit, which had so successfully conducted special forces operations against the British joined the Germans even before the establishment of Mussolini's "republic". See Greene and Massignani, *The Black Prince*. The RSI navy, during its short existence, clashed at least forty times with Allied coastal units and conducted attacks against larger warships like destroyers.

[57] Roskill. *War at Sea*, 83.

Florence by early August. That same month American and French units invaded France's Riviera coast. Germany's Mediterranean controlled shoreline contracted dramatically, but it did not disappear. By the fall of 1944 the situation had stabilized once again, leaving Germany in possession of the Italian ports of La Spezia, Genoa, Imperia's harbors of Oneglia and Puerto Maurizo, and San Remo. Thus, the naval war continued. In fact, compressing the operational zone seemed to intensify the action.

By September 1944 von Gartzen's 10th Flotilla could muster *TA24*, *TA28*, *TA29*, *TA31* and *TA32*. In general these were modern Italian torpedo boats, which had been nearing completion at the time of the Italian armistice. They displaced 1,130 tons full load, could steam at twenty-eight knots and carried a pair of 3.9-inch/47 guns and six 17.7-inch torpedoes. *TA32*, however, was the ex-Yugoslavian destroyer *Dubrovnik* (ex-Italian *Premuda*). She displaced about 2,800 tons and, as rearmed by the Germans, carried four 4.1-inch/45 guns and three 21-inch torpedoes.[58]

THE GERMAN VIEW

On the evening of 1 October 1944 von Gartzen departed Genoa aboard *TA24*. *TA29* and *TA32* followed, loaded with a total of ninety-eight mines on deck rails. He was to meet four MFP (armed barges) and three R-boat (motor-minesweepers) and then lay a defensive minefield off San Remo, a base for German and Italian motor torpedo boats.[59] Mine-laying was a nerve-wracking job that destroyer men dreaded. One British admiral called it "unpleasant work for a naval man, an occupation like that of rat-catching."[60] A few well-aimed shells, even an accident, could detonate the cargo and wipe out a ship's crew.

As the Germans steamed west along the Italian Rivera the night was bright and visibility good, the sky swept clean by a stiff breeze blowing off the sea. At 2200 the R-boats joined up and ranged ahead of the larger

---

[58] See Freivogel, "Siluranti ex Italiane Sotto Bandiera Tedesca." Hervieux, "German TA Torpedo Boats at War." Ship's data is extracted from Bagnasco and Cernuschi, *Le navi da Guerra italiane*.

[59] The MFP (*Marinefährprahm*) were landing craft that could transport 200 soldiers or 140 tons of supplies and also came in gunboat versions. R-boats (*Räumboote*) displaced between 120-150 tons, depending upon the type, could make 21-25 knots and carried up to one 37-mm gun, six 20-mm guns and ten mines.

[60] Lott, Most Dangerous Sea, 17.

warships. (The MFPs were delayed and failed to make the rendezvous.) Minutes later von Gartzen received an urgent radio message that enemy warships had been observed in the exact zone he was supposed to mine.[61]

Despite this intelligence, the German force continued on course. It was 2300 and they had just passed Imperia—shore-based radio intelligence was continuing to warn of enemy ships—when lookouts aboard *TA24* spotted a large, two-funneled vessel about eleven-thousand yards to the southwest. Six minutes later they reported two smaller warships in the distance behind the first contact. They identified the large ship as a French light cruiser, not a vessel any destroyer would care to tangle with, much less ones loaded with mines. As the lookouts nervously monitored the situation, the cruiser turned to port and assumed a parallel course. Von Gartzen continued west hoping the mountainous shoreline beyond his ships would confuse enemy radar and make his force hard to see. However, at 2320 a salvo of six to eight rounds, fired from what spotters identified as twin-barreled mounts, fell around *TA24*, some shells splashing only fifty yards off.

The German ships maneuvered wildly as the next salvo targeted *TA29*. Von Gartzen withheld fire, not wanting to reveal his position, and the range was too great to permit a torpedo counterattack. His drop zone remained fourteen nautical miles ahead and mine-laying, especially off a friendly port, required slow speeds and precise navigation. He also worried about the R-boats up ahead and did not want to expose them to danger by increasing speed and trying to evade in their direction. For these reasons, the German commander decided to scrub the mission and ordered a simultaneous turn to starboard. *TA24* swung about but *TA29* continued ahead, the mines making her response to her helm sluggish. She rammed *TA24* at a 90 degree angle, her bow grinding six feet into the other ship's side. For a dreadful minute the two ships remained locked together before *TA29* managed to separate by backing her engines. *TA24* suffered rudder damage and a flooded shaft tunnel while water inundated one of *TA29*'s forward compartments. It could have been far worse.

---

[61] This account is based on Wirich Von Gartzen. *Die Flottille Außergewöhnlicher Seekrieg deutscher Mittelmeer-Torpedoboote* and the SKL War Diary, 1 October 1944 (Both courtesy of Peter M. Kreuzer)

After milling around and then regaining formation, the Germans fled east, hugging the shoreline. *TA24* took the rear position to guard her laden companions. At 2334 von Gartzen gave his gunners permission to return fire. The 3.9-inch guns ranged in on their target, which now bore thirteen thousand yards to the south-southwest. They ripped out a salvo and then another. Lookouts "perfectly observed" two shells striking home. There was a dense cloud of smoke. The cruiser ceased fire and continued west, breaking contact. The other two enemy vessels seemed to follow. The Germans were surprised by this turn of events and supposed they had inflicted serious damage on the enemy.

The 10th made Genoa at 0215 on 2 October without further adventure, their mines still aboard.

The three R-boats continued their mission. Two hours later they experienced inaccurate gunfire, but this caused no damage and they succeeded in sowing their mines in a "favorable alternative position" south of Bordighera. The SKL war diary noted: "Torpedo Boat engagement off Imperia with probable French cruiser and large destroyer. Two hits were perfectly observed on the opponents. Use of torpedoes was not possible due to distance." Later historians noted this entry and some mentioned the engagement.[62] However, French records indicated that none of their vessels were operating in the area that night.

THE CIVILIAN VIEW

Von Gartzen's brief battle did not pass unnoticed ashore. Carcello Carli, an Italian civilian, lived near the coastal cliffs west of Imperia. He was at home with his family and some German soldiers quartered in their house. At about 2330 he heard sudden gunfire out to sea. Despite the curfew, Carli and his father ran into their garden, which overlooked the ocean. They saw flashes from a ship that seemed several miles offshore shooting toward the south-southeast. After a few minutes they observed three dark silhouettes surrounded by geysers heading east hugging the coast. Carli remembered: "At that moment we heard the engines of an air-

---

[62] It seemed that the 'unknown' destroyer (or light cruiser) was hit twice by *TA24*'s fire." Hervieux, "German TA Torpedo Boats at War," 140.

craft and at the same time the dark night (the whole town was in total darkness) turned into day due to star shells (I did not know whether the stars came from the aircraft or were shot by the ship), In this light, which lasted about a minute, we could see the three ships just in front of us while the aircraft dropped a few bombs over them."

The three silhouettes disappeared to the east, apparently unharmed. Carli recalled that the German batteries around Imperia remained silent. He always wondered what he had seen, but it took sixty years to find out.[63]

ALLIED ORGANIZATION AND PREOCCUPATIONS

The U.S. Navy contributed Task Force 86 commanded by Rear Admiral Lyal. A. Davidson to a formation called Flank Force Mediterranean. Its missions were to patrol the waters off the western portion of the German held coast, suppress German naval activity and, as S. E. Morison described it, to "keep the coastal batteries along the Italian Riviera stirred up."[64] Davidson rotated two cruisers, *Brooklyn* and *Philadelphia,* and various destroyers into and out of this force. The French contributed Cruiser Division 3 under Rear Admiral Philippe Auboyneau, consisting of the light cruisers *Georges Leygues, Montcalm* and *Gloire*. The old French battleship *Lorraine* stood available should any target worthy of her guns (and the risk of taking such a large and slow ship into enemy-infested waters) appear. Davidson also deployed one American and two British motor torpedo-boat squadrons and a flock of minesweepers, sub chasers and patrol craft: sufficient force to dominate a 200-mile stretch of enemy held coast and harass coastal batteries.

The Allies worried, however, about small battle units possessed by the Germans that would, theoretically, offset their overwhelming preponderances in strength.[65] These were cheap and expendable special weapons like explosive boats and manned torpedoes that had the potential to inflict great harm—as demonstrated by the fates of *Queen Elizabeth* and *Valiant,*

---

[63] Carcello Carli, Correspondence with the author, September 2005.

[64] Morison, *Invasion of France and Germany.* 311.

[65] *Ibid.* Even though this type of weapon failed to inflict much damage in the target rich environment off Normandy in June and July.

sunk by Italian manned torpedoes, and *Tirpitz*, severely damaged by British miniature submarines

Two flotillas of *Linsen* explosive boats arrived at San Remo in early September followed by two flotillas of *Marder* manned torpedoes and one of *Molch* miniature submarines.[66] The Allies—forewarned by intelligence of their deployment in the Ligurian Gulf—alerted their ships to be prepared to meet this threat. Their first encounter with small battle units occurred on 5 September when a flotilla of *Marder* attacked the French destroyer *Le Malin* and the USS *Ludlow*. After a "spirited hunt [which] developed as the Perspex domes of the human torpedoes began appearing on all sides of the destroyers," the Allied ships destroyed three *Marder* and captured their crews.[67] More encounters followed: PTs engaged a *Linsen* explosive control boat and its drones on 10 September and again on the 16th.[68] On the night of 25-26 September a dozen *Molch*, each one armed with a pair of torpedoes slung to its side, attacked Allied shipping from their base at San Remo, but only two returned. Nonetheless, this type of unit, by their insidious and semi-kamikaze nature, seemed more "alarming" and, as subsequent events demonstrated, they seemed to occupy the minds of American sailors more than ordinary, but much more deadly weapons, like mines or destroyers.

1 October 1944 turned out to be a busy day for the Flank Force, particularly the Benson class destroyer USS *Gleaves* skippered by Commander W. M. Klee (2,395 tons, 4 x 5-inch/38-caliber guns, 5 x 21-inch torpedo tubes, 35 knots). *Gleaves* began the day patrolling south of San Remo with USS *Benson* and *PT308*. At 0500 these warships left for other duties. At 0724 *Gleaves* depth-charged an overturned fishing boat. At 0850 she stood off Imperia and bombarded a ship outside the Oneglia breakwater, dodging the return fire of Imperia's shore batteries for ten minutes. At 0938 she discovered and sank a floating mine.[69] USS *Brooklyn*, anchored at San Tropez, France provided reconnaissance services with her four float planes and at 0950 they reported MAS boats (small Italian motor

---

[66] See Roskill, *War at Sea*, II, 101 and 454-55 for particulars of the Small Battle Units.

[67] Tomblin. *With Utmost Spirit,* 448.

[68] See Bulkley, *At Close Quarters* , 335-36.

[69] USS *Gleaves*. "Action Report: Dragoon Operation," 13

torpedo boats), a merchant vessel, a tanker and a tug in San Remo, Porto Maurizio and Oneglia.[70] At 1020 *Gleaves* was back off Imperia and there she stayed for the next ninety minutes, sending 230 five-inch rounds crashing into Porto Maurizio and Oneglia harbors and claiming one hit on a coastal steamer and two probable hits on a barge. Meanwhile, *Benson* pounded the MAS boats in San Remo. After a break *Gleaves* appeared off Cape Martola at 1727 and dueled with the shore battery there, expending 196 5-inch rounds. Meanwhile, a blustery wind blowing onshore from the Ligurian Sea began rising from thirty to forty-five knots. This sent the PT boats heading for port. With the fall of darkness *Gleaves* began patrolling along a line five miles long, zigzagging at fifteen knots in a south-southeast, north-northwest direction, standing closer to shore to compensate for the lack of PT coverage.

The American View

It had been an active day, but hopes that the night would be quieter were disappointed when news arrived that Allied aircraft had bombed three enemy vessels off Porto Maurizio at 2107. Klee decided to cruise toward Imperia to look for these intruders. At 2255 *Gleaves* made a possible radar contact off Porto Maurizio. By 2313 Klee was tracking a line of three units heading west-southwest along the coast. At 2319 the American destroyer swung around to the southwest on a parallel course, rang up twenty knots and opened fire at an estimated range of 10,900 yards using, as Klee reported, "radar rangers and bearings, rocking ladder of two hundred yards in fifty yard steps, concentrating on center ship."[71]

At 2321 *Gleaves* increased speed to twenty-five knots as the targets seemed to be sailing at twenty-two knots—much faster than originally estimated. At 2324 the American ceased fire and observed the enemy ships circling in a small area. The destroyer's five-inch guns lashed out with another broadside. Two minutes later, unidentified lights suddenly illuminated the area—presumably flares dropped by an aircraft. *Gleaves* shot very lights to identify herself as an Allied ship, lest she come under friendly attack. Three minutes after that, Klee reported "the targets were now in-

---

[70] USS *Brooklyn.* "Action Report, Operation Dragoon.

[71] USS *Gleaves* Report of Surface Actions with German Forces, 3 October 1944, 2.

distinct and situation was very obscure."[72] *Gleaves* slowed to ten knots and fired a spread of star shells, but all these showed was a dense cloud of smoke close inshore where the contacts had been.

Although there was nothing to see, radar indicated at least one ship fleeing east. Klee came to port and rang up twenty knots. Lookouts spotted a large explosion from within the smoky area. He ordered more star shells in a vain attempt to visualize events. Then, at 2335, enemy fire suddenly erupted. One shell splashed in the destroyer's vicinity and Klee assumed that German shore batteries had joined the action. Four minutes later radar reported two aircraft only three miles away. *Gleaves* made smoke and headed downwind under this protection, away from the action, more worried about a possible friendly air attack. The enemy gunfire tapered off within six minutes and at 2348 Klee secured from general quarters. His ship had expended eighty rounds of AA common and eight star shells during the brief action. He knew at least one enemy ship was escaping east, but was content to let it go. In his report the captain concluded he had bombarded three merchant ships. He claimed two of them had exploded under fire and had sunk or been seriously damaged.

Subsequent events that night overshadowed the importance of this confusing and unsatisfactory encounter in the minds of captain and crew.

At 0209 on 3 October *Gleaves* pinged a pair of small targets off Cape San Stefano assessed as "two enemy coastal steamers."[73] She engaged at 0225 and expended ninety rounds of common and sixteen stars before observing "explosion similar to that observed during the first attack."[74] The destroyer lofted a spread of star shells and saw a lot of smoke, but nothing else. Radar likewise showed clear so *Gleaves* secured from general quarters once again and turned west toward her original patrol line, leaving her targets, the mine laden R-boats, still in the area—silhouettes and radar signatures hidden against the dark shore. The explosion observed by *Gleaves* was, like the first one, wishful thinking as the Germans described her gunfire as inaccurate.

---

[72] Ibid.

[73] USS *Gleaves* War Diary October 1-31, 1944, 1.

[74] USS *Gleaves*, Report of Surface Actions, 3.

By 0327 *Gleaves* was approaching her original patrol area when the port lookout warned of a wake approaching from ahead. As the claxon sounded general quarters once again the officer of the deck swung the ship hard-a-port and the wake passed astern. Then lookouts spotted a small boat about a thousand yards off the starboard beam. *Gleaves* heeled in a hard circle to port as the boat slipped down the starboard side and passed only twenty yards astern, bobbing in the destroyer's wake. Machine guns and the main battery opened up and at 0333 the craft, a German explosive boat, exploded.

As *Gleaves* left the area two more explosive boats appeared off her port bow. The destroyer ran past them, but they turned and followed off either quarter. *Gleaves* dropped depth charges in her wake. Only one detonated, but this caused a boat to veer out of control. Both MTBs exploded at 0346. In this action the destroyer expended seven 5-inch, 140 20-mm, twenty 40-mm rounds and three depth charges.[75]

Gleaves circled back after dawn and rescued two operators floating in the sea. One confessed to being "chagrined at having missed."[76] *Gleaves* also found an abandoned boat that she hoisted on deck. For this prize the commanders of Cruiser Division Eight and the Commander of the Eighth Fleet both congratulated the destroyer and recommended a slew of medals for her crew.

---

[75] USS *Gleaves*. "Capture of Enemy Personnel and Vessel", 3.
[76] *Ibid.*, 4.

CONCLUSION

The German, American and Italian accounts of this mystery battle off Imperia match closely, given the different points of reference, but all missed the big picture, although the Germans came closest. They at least correctly identified their opponent as a warship, although they magnified its size, and added two phantom destroyers for good measure. They, like the Americans, incorrectly claimed they damaged their enemy. They failed to accomplish their mission, but even if the reasons were not quite as compelling as reported, they were still good enough.

The Americans made a series of wrong assumptions starting with their opposition, which Klee assessed as merchant ships, despite strong evidence to the contrary, including their high speed and the fact they fired back. On the basis of an explosion observed aboard *Gleaves*, but not ashore or by the Germans, the destroyer concluded she had damaged or destroyed her target(s) and took this as reason to prematurely terminate the action.[77] In fact, *Gleaves* had the 10th Torpedo Boat Flotilla cornered and at a serious disadvantage. But Captain Klee, more concerned with the threat of friendly aircraft, permitted the enemy to escape rather than aggressively pursuing and seeking a battle of elimination.

The story of this encounter stands as an example of how expectations of enemy activities mixed with fog of war influenced the course and the later assessments of events. The German and U.S. navies fought a battle off the Italian coast. Both sides misidentified their opponent. Events like the brush with the Axis small battle units and even aircraft flying overhead seemed more pertinent to the American destroyer. Both sides filed action reports, which justified their actions and which, naturally, dominated the historical record.

How important was this brief action? In the total scope of the war, it was insignificant. In terms of the Ligurian Campaign, the lost opportunity carried more weight. The 10th Torpedo Boat Flotilla remained a thorn in the side of the Allied navies, tying down a much larger force, and sinking at least six ships with their mines after 2 October. Not until March 1945

---

[77] The captain recorded an explosion in the second of the *Gleaves*'s three engagements that night, the one against the R-boats, and considered it sufficient cause to terminate his attack as well.

did three British destroyers finally run the 10th Flotilla down during the course of another mining mission and sank *T24* and *T29* in the European Theater's last naval surface engagement.[78]

---

[78] See O'Hara, *German Fleet at War*, 245-47 and Hervieux, *TA Boats at War,* 138 for ships sunk and 147-48 for the last surface action.

CHAPTER 6. THE NAVAL WAR OFF SYRIA: THE ROYAL NAVY FIGHTS THE MARINE NATIONALE, JUNE 1941

By the spring of 1941 the British Empire appeared to be losing the war. In February Axis armies led by General Erwin Rommel had reconquered Cyrenaica in Italian North Africa after London unwisely diverted four divisions to Greece. Then Germany routed this small expeditionary force in April and grabbed Crete in an audacious airborne assault in May. The Royal Navy evacuating its beaten army suffered staggering losses including four cruisers, six destroyers, and thirty small craft. In addition, Axis forces damaged three battleships, an aircraft-carrier, six cruisers, and seven destroyers. In the Atlantic, the sinking of *Bismarck* proved a costly victory that did little to reverse the course of the critical mercantile war. Axis U-boats, surface raiders and aircraft continued to inflict an ever-growing toll while the need to support the North African army by transporting men and supplies ten thousand miles around Africa placed an unsupportable burden on Britain's hard-pressed merchant marine. The home front especially suffered. The government imposed rationing in March 1940 and by April 1941 imports had dropped to barely half what they had been then. With the conquest of Yugoslavia and Greece, London's last two European allies, the British Empire truly stood alone.

London counted among its enemies its erstwhile ally, the French State, more commonly known as Vichy France after the name of its capital located in the southern, unoccupied territory. The perception that France, at this difficult moment in its history, was a German puppet is common, but incorrect. France still controlled its empire, the world's second largest, and the French Fleet remained intact—a powerful force with high morale under the command of Admiral Jean-François Darlan. The Reich could not bully France past a certain point lest the fleet and the colonies rejoined the Allies. The consequences of that event, as the German Grand Admiral Erich Raeder explained to Hitler in a March 1941 memorandum would be dire: "Every bridgehead in Africa would be lost ... All anti-Axis forces in the world would be given fresh encouragement both politically and propagandistically. France would be missing when it comes to rebuilding Europe."[79] However, Raeder continued, if France could be induced to become an Axis partner, "it would be a great political success with far-reaching effects. For all practical purposes Europe would be united against the Anglo-Americans. It is hardly necessary to mention that it might be of the greatest importance if French forces, particularly the fleet, could be induced to go beyond the tasks of defending French interests and to attack British positions, British supply lines, etc."[80]

The sorry state of Anglo-French relations was a consequence of British suspicions. The June 1940 armistice specified that French navy ships "except that part left free for the safeguard of French interests in the Colonial Empire, are to be collected in ports to be specified, demobilized, and disarmed under German or Italian control."81 Naturally, London distrusted this arrangement as well as Darlan's subsequent assurances that his fleet would never enter the war on the Axis side. The only certainty was that if the Axis controlled the French fleet the Royal Navy would find itself facing an enemy nearly its equal—a completely unthinkable situation for Churchill, the Sea Lords and the public. To prevent this outcome Churchill acted to seize or neutralize as many French warships as possible. The attack of the Royal Navy's Force H on the powerful French Force de Raid anchored at Mers-el Kébir, and the deaths of 1,297 French sailors in that action, marked the most extreme expression of Churchill's decision. As the New York Times editorialized three days later: "If the order to fire on the ships of its former ally portended nothing else, it would remove the last doubt of Britain's determination to fight on. It would never have cut the last tie with the French except as grim prelude to a battle to the death."

In September 1940 Great Britain attempted to seize the strategic French colonial port of Dakar in West Africa. In a three day naval siege, the battleship *Richelieu*, shore batteries and submarines sent the British packing after nearly sinking the battleship *Resolution*. Following Dakar, with French honor restored, the ex-allies backed away from the brink of open warfare. The Royal Navy and *Marine Nationale* reached an unspoken

---

[79] Showell, *Fuehrer Conferences,* 188.

[80] *Ibid.,* 189.

[81] Page, *Royal Navy and the Mediterranean,* 29.

modus operandi whereby the British respected superior French forces and French ships in port, but everything else remained fair game. France could operate within these limits and from the fall of 1940, when it ran its first convoy through the Straits of Gibraltar, few incidents occurred.

Figure 39. Admiral Jean-François Darlan. As commander of the French navy he was not known for his pro-British views even before the Royal Navy's attack on the French fleet at Mers el-Kebir in July 1940. (Musée de la Marine, Paris)

Germany monitored Anglo-French tensions with great interest and barely concealed hope. A fresh opportunity to enlist France into the Axis cause came in April 1941 when an anti-British government seized power in Iraq and appealed for assistance. On 9 May German aircraft landed in Syria (French concessions in this matter being matched by German concessions in armistice and occupation conditions) on their way to Mosul. On 11 May Admiral Darlan met with Hitler, bringing Great Britain's mistrust of French intentions to a boil. And with reason. Darlan, along with most of the world, believed that Germany would win the war. By courting Hitler he sought the best possible outcome for France in the peace that would follow. He did not like the Germans any more than he liked the British (and he was a self-described Anglophobe) but he was a realist.

Figure 40. Hitler and Darlan shaking hands during their meeting of May 11, 1941. This was one of the events which alarmed London and led to the decision to invade Syria. (University of Stuttgart, *Chronology of the War at Sea*)

Churchill signaled his commander in the Middle East, General Sir Archibald Wavell: "Our information leads us to believe that Admiral Darlan has probably made some bargain to help the Germans to get in [Syria]."[82] In fact, Churchill was reading Enigma intercepts. As the official British history on intelligence noted:

> "From 14 May, when the Enigma had confirmed the arrival of (German Air Force) aircraft in Syria, en route for Iraq, Whitehall became convinced that German would move into Syria unless she was forestalled by early British action. On 19 May, when the attack on Crete was expected hourly and the position in Iraq had not yet been secured, they instructed Wavell to improvise the largest possible force for a movement into Syria at the earliest possible moment."[83]

Accordingly, Australian, Indian and Free French units began massing in Palestine. On 15 and 18 May the British bombed French airfields at Palmyra and Damascus. Simultaneously, operations against the Iraqi Arab

---

[82] Churchill, *Grand Alliance*, 289.

[83] Hinsley, *British Intelligence*, 85.

government proceeded and in just a few weeks Great Britain conquered Iraq in a boldly conducted campaign, capturing some German airmen in the process. By 30 May the threat seemed over, especially as France ordered all Germans out of Syria. On 1 June the German foreign minister Joachim von Ribbentrop declared a British invasion of Syria was "completely impossible." By this time the focus of Hitler's attention had passed over France as he waited the unleashing of what von Ribbentrop hinted to French representatives would be momentous events in the east. German intelligence seemed likewise distracted because they were surprised when on 8 June 1941 an Allied force, consisting of the 7th Australian Division, part of the 1st Cavalry Division, the 5th Indian Brigade and a Free French Brigade invaded Syria.

The British fielded 34,000 troops, inferior to the French strength of approximately 50,000. The official Australian history commented that the campaign, "fought in a country with a restricted coastal corridor and a vital coast road with long stretches in full view from the sea, was ideal for naval cooperation."[84] The plan, accordingly, envisioned a quick thrust up the coastal road by the Australian 21st Brigade assisted by an amphibious landing at the mouth of the Litani River to secure an important bridge. The French could realistically only hope for major reinforcements via the sea. This meant that the British, despite their inferior numbers, could secure their objective by conquering the coast and imposing a naval blockade.

The French naval force available to contest the Allied attack and maintain communications with France consisted of the large destroyers *Guépard* (division flag of Capitaine de Vaisseau Raymond Gervais de Lafond), *Valmy*, the sloop *Élan* and three submarines, *Caïman, Morse*, and *Souffleur*. The French destroyers, while seriously outnumbered by their immediate opposition, enjoyed some advantages. They were large, displacing 3,200 tons full load, and capable of thirty-five knots. Their 5.45-inch guns fired a shell larger even than some of the British light cruisers. They also carried six 21.7-inch torpedoes.

---

[84] Gill, *Australian Navy I.* 378.

Figure 41. The 2400 tonnes class contre-torpilleur *Guépard.* These large, fast, and heavily armed vessels demonstrated the practicality of their design off Syria. She survived the Syrian campaign only to be scuttled in Toulon in November 1942 (Courtesy of John Jordan)

Figure 42. The contre-torpilleur *Valmy.* She was also scuttled in Toulon in November 1942 and salvaged by the Italians as *FR24.* (Courtesy of John Jordan)

The British initially deployed Force B with the cruisers *Phoebe* and *Ajax* and destroyers *Kandahar, Kimberley, Jackal,* and *Janus,* and Force C with the cruiser *Coventry,* the destroyers *Ilex, Isis, Hotspur, Hero,* and the landing ship *Glengyle* and all under the command of Vice Admiral E.L.S. King at Haifa in Palestine. The British "I"- and "H"-class destroyers displaced about 1,850 tons full load and had four 4.7 guns, eight 21-inch torpedo tubes and could steam at thirty-six knots under ideal conditions. The "J" and "K" classes were larger: 2,330 tons with six 4.7-inch guns and ten 21-inch torpedo tubes.

Early on 8 June the first attempt to land British commandos failed due to heavy surf. Although the commandos were willing to go in, *Glengyle*'s captain judged the bright moonlight dangerous and canceled the operation. Later that morning Australian troops crossed the border. By afternoon they had captured the first objective, the ancient city of Tyre. Their next objective was the Khan Bridge over the Litani River. The brigade's advanced elements closed up to the river only to find the bridge blown and strong French resistance. Accordingly, the *Glengyle* returned at 3:00 a.m. on June 9, just at moonset, and sent 395 men of the 11th (Scottish) Commando ashore in eleven landing craft. Two detachments made the north shore as planned. The most northerly group attacked the Kafr Badda Bridge two miles further north and captured it. The center detachment attempted to occupy a French barrack. The main party, however, missed the river's mouth due to a sand bar and landed on the wrong side. When they tried to cross north to support their comrades, heavy artillery and machine gun fire pinned them down. The memories of one commando, Jimmy Lappin, summarized the situation. "We had just cleared the beach and were lying in scrub grass. It was just after dawn on a beautiful clear morning. The air was still and when I looked over to the next two blokes, MacKay and Hurst, a couple of yards away, they had just lit up cigarettes. I could see two thin columns of blue smoke rising and I thought that I would have a smoke too but, just as I got my cigarettes out, the whistle blew for us to advance. These two blokes never moved, they were both hit, the smoke gave away their position."[85] French armored cars counterattacked and drove back the northern commando group that afternoon. The center group proved too weak to repulse French charges from the barracks and suffered heavy losses, including the commanding officer. Overall, fifty-four men died or were taken prisoner while fifty were wounded.

---

[85] http://www.combinedops.com/Black%20Hackle.htm

Figure 43. HMS *Kimberley* in May 1941. The J and K classes broke with earlier British destroyer designs having six 4.7-inch guns in twin mounts and ten torpedo tubes, although one bank was landed in favor of a 4-inch antiaircraft weapon. (National Maritime Museum London)

Figure 44. The minesweeping sloop *Élan*. She displaced 895 tons full load and was armed with a pair of 3.9-in guns. These ships served in the Italian, German, British, and Free French navies. (Du-gardin.com)

When news of the landing reached Beirut at 0900 de Lafond's division sortied. Appearing on the scene an hour later, the destroyers engaged an Australian column marching up the coast road south of the Litani River. They lacked high explosive ammunition for their guns, however, which would have been more deadly against ground targets than the armor piecing shells available and, coming under counter-fire from an Australian artillery battery, they withdrew after expending sixty rounds.

When Vice-Admiral King heard the French naval bombardment he led *Phoebe* and *Ajax* toward the Litani River at full speed. However, he arrived too late to catch de Lafond. In fact, he almost got caught himself because at 1206 *Caïman* barely missed *Ajax* with a torpedo salvo. (She thought she had the battleship *Barham* in her crosshairs).[86] Admiral King then ordered four destroyers to sweep north along the coast while he retired toward Haifa. In addition to the submarine danger, he had experienced first hand off Crete the destructive potential of air attacks against ships and the day before, French Morane 406 fighters based out of Rayack, Lebanon had shot down three Fulmars of the Fleet Air Arm, and damaging two more.[87]

Figure 45. British Fulmer over a Mediterranean convoy. These naval fighters were easy prey for French fighters. (IWM A3793)

Patrolling off Sidon, de Lafond sighted King's destroyers at 1335. *Janus*, the flag of the senior officer, Commander J. A. W. Tothill, sailed in the lead with *Jackal* about a mile off her starboard quarter; *Hotspur* followed one mile behind *Jackal*. *Isis* provided fire support inshore, two

---

[86] Antier, Jean-Jacques, *Batailles Navales*, 1,115.

[87] Page, *Royal Navy and the Mediterranean.* 122.

miles south of *Hotspur*. Tothill ordered his flotilla to attack and turned toward the enemy but, being so spread out, concerted action was initially impossible. Under Tothill's rules of engagement, imposed by an Admiralty still anxious to limit hostilities, he could not fire first. However, he expected the French would close range before beginning any hostile action, giving time to concentrate his ships. But de Lafond surprised Tothill when the first salvos splashed nearby shortly after. *Janus* could not reply until 1343 when the range had closed to fifteen thousand yards. Exploiting his temporary advantage in numbers, de Lafond pressed on and eight minutes later, now shooting from ten thousand yards, *Guépard* landed three shells on *Janus* in quick succession. The first blew a hole in the aft deck. The next exploded outside the captain's sea cabin, killing everyone on the bridge except Tothill. The third slammed into No. 1 boiler room and destroyed the saturated steam pipe. With steam escaping and No. 2 boiler also out of action, the British destroyer lost headway. As she drifted to a stop two more shells piled in: a dud jolted her port fan intake and, finally, a fifth hit inflicted further damage in No. 1 boiler room. *Janus* dropped smoke floats and worked her guns under local control, rolling on the swell.

At this juncture, *Jackal* arrived, spewing smoke which she proceeded to wrap around her stricken sister. Then she turned to port to open her broadside and at 1400 sent three torpedoes churning on a long run north. For the next twelve minutes the two sides swapped salvoes until *Guépard* and *Valmy* maneuvered away to avoid *Jackal's* "fish" and started making smoke of their own. *Jackal* went to full speed, zigzagging to present a difficult target. *Hotspur* followed twenty-five hundred yards astern while *Isis* lagged a mile behind *Hotspur*. The French presented broadsides and opened fire once again, range eleven thousand yards. *Jackal* turned parallel and replied; then a 5.45-inch shell exploded on *Jackal's* upper deck igniting a small blaze in the tiller flat and wounding one man.

Figure 46. Reloading the 5.45 (138-mm) gun which armed the French contre-
torpilleurs. This weapon could fire an 89.5-lb shell to a range of nearly 22,000
yards at a rate of seven rounds a minute. (Paul Carré)

After striking this blow de Lafond steered north putting some more distance between his ships and the enemy so as to exploit the advantage of
his heavier guns. At 1440 he turned again, flung a few salvos and then re-
sumed course for Beirut. The British called off the chase about ten miles
short of Beirut. *Jackal* expended 611 4.7-inch rounds, but *Guépard* suffered only minor splinter damage from near misses.

This destroyer action represented an impressive performance against
experienced British units on the open sea. *Kimberley* towed *Janus* to Haifa
where she burned out of control until 0500 the next day. She did not return
to action until March 1942. The Admiralty concluded *Janus* should not
have engaged without the support of her mates and conceded that the long
range gunnery of the French destroyers clearly surpassed their own abili-
ties.

Figure 47. The New Zealand light cruiser *Leander*. She chased the French contre-torpilleurs on several occasions but was never able to bring them under her guns. *Leander* went on to serve in the Pacific and was torpedoed by Japanese destroyers at the battle of Kolombargara in July 1943. (copyright holder unknown)

Over the next several days King's squadron underwent some changes. On 10 June the 10th Destroyer Flotilla comprising *Stuart*, *Jaguar*, *Griffin* and *Defender* arrived, followed on the 13th by the New Zealand cruiser *Leander* and the destroyers *Jervis* and *Hasty*. Meanwhile, *Ajax*, *Stuart*, *Hotspur* and *Kandahar* all departed. King's primary missions were to prevent reinforcements and to speed the coastal advance by delivering fire support as needed. One of *Leander*'s men described the process:

> "Watching with binoculars, we saw enemy transports hammering downhill in clouds of dust ... We caught the leading transport emerging into dusty sunlight, followed swiftly by several more driving madly, then, straight into burst after burst of thirty to forty direct hits along the lower stretch of coastal road. Trucks lazily leapt upward to disintegrate, while others careered off the highway ... before crashing over shallow cliffs onto the rocks below. Greyish [sic] white puffs along clifftops indicated retaliation from French 75-mm. guns, followed by large water spouts close among our destroyers."[88]

De Lafond's small squadron remained active despite overwhelming odds. His destroyers conducted "tip and run" raids, trying to catch isolated British ships and getting in some licks of their own against enemy ground forces. On 14 June *Leander* and *Coventry* got word of *Guépard* and *Valmy* to the north. Accompanied by four destroyers the Allied cruisers hurried to

---

[88] Halker, *Well Done Leander*, 140.

intercept and by 1635 *Leander* had the enemy in sight. But the French ships fled to the protection of Beirut's 9.2-inch batteries before the cruisers could bring them to action.

Figure 48. Valmy dodging British salvos during the June 10th action. (from Historique de la Marine française Darrieus and Quéguiner)

The Australian 21st Brigade captured Sidon on 15 June and their drive bogged down against stiffening resistance. German aircraft, meanwhile, flying from newly won Aegean bases, joined French planes in making King's coastal forays even more dangerous. On 15 June 15 at 1703 German Ju-88s jumped the destroyer *Isis*. An observer aboard *Leander* saw one Ju-88 plunge from above "with siren screaming ... flashing through bursting shells and ribbons of tracer." Her bomb exploded close alongside. "Watching in awe, I saw daylight below (the destroyer's) keel, and then her stern rose slowly from the mass of churning sea and blanket of black smoke."[89] Two hours later a formation of sixteen French Glen Martin bombers near missed *Ilex* with two 500-lb bombs and opened her No. 1 boiler room to the sea. This knocked both destroyers out of action for more than a year.

Admiral Darlan, meanwhile, reacted angrily to the British invasion. His second in command dissuaded him from ordering the entire French fleet to

---

[89] *Ibid.*, 145.

sail from Toulon. He settled for a much smaller effort. On June 11 the "super" destroyer *Chevalier Paul* departed Toulon carrying eight hundred much needed rounds of 5.45-inch ammunition. She passed the Italian Aegean Island of Castellorizo on 15 June hugging the Turkish coast to make the dangerous passage around Cypress at night. However, because the French needed to ask German approval for the sailing, Enigma told the British she was coming. Knowing where to look, a reconnaissance aircraft spotted *Chevalier Paul* at 1815 and a flight of six Swordfish departed Cypress to attack. At 0300 on 16 June they found her under the light of a bright moon. The destroyer shot down one Swordfish, but the slow biwing bombers pressed on and a torpedo smashed against the French warship's hull and opened it to uncontrollable flooding. *Chevalier Paul* radioed for help and within an hour *Valmy* and *Guépard* had steam up and departed Beirut to render aid. They had barely cleared the port, however, when they encountered *Leander*, *Jervis*, and *Kimberley* sailing up the coast. Leery of French long-range gunnery, *Kimberley* came to full speed and charged the French ships as both sides opened fire. De Lafond's orders did not call for him to engage a superior foe (he was nearly out of ammunition in any case) so he made smoke and turned back to Beirut. In the brief engagement the French destroyers expended seventy-eight 5.45-inch rounds while *Kimberley* claimed hits, but in fact neither side damaged the other. Once the Allied ships departed, hurried off by French aircraft which unsuccessfully bombed *Kimberley*, *Guépard* and *Valmy* set out once again. But they arrived too late. *Chevalier Paul* sank at 0645 and all they could do was rescue survivors (including the crew of the downed Swordfish).

Meanwhile, Admiral A. B. Cunningham, commander of the Mediterranean Fleet based in Alexandria, Egypt, continued to reinforce King. On 17 June the cruiser *Naid* and the destroyers *Kingston*, *Jaguar*, and *Nizam* joined his squadron. However, disturbed by the growing number of ships under repair, and faced with a stalemated ground campaign, Cunningham ordered King to remain in Haifa during daylight hours rather than risk German and French air attacks.

On 18 June the sloop *Élan* bombarded Allied positions along the coast. The "super" destroyer *Vauquelin* reached Beirut on 21 June carrying eight hundred 5.45-inch rounds, but British bombers damaged her in port the next day. *Vauquelin*'s fate demonstrated the danger of lingering in Beirut and the French naval commander determined his fleet should disperse at night when French fighters could not provide cover.

Figure 49. Crew of *Chevalier Paul* crowding aboard *Guépard*. (from *Historique de la Marine française* Darrieus and Quéguiner)

On 19 June French ground forces counterattacked and recaptured Mezze outside Damascus, forcing the surrender of two Indian and one British battalion. But on 21 June Australian forces broke through and occupied Damascus after intense combat. Another British column entered the country from Iraq, but a company of Foreign Legionnaires held them up outside Palmyra.

On the night of 22 June *Guépard* and *Valmy* slipped their moorings leaving the damaged *Vauquelin* at dock. Steaming north-northwest at eight knots (to conserve fuel) de Lafond intended to pass the night loitering four to ten miles off Ras Beyrouth. Six miles north of the city lookouts reported unexpected silhouettes looming out of the dark. He had run into an enemy squadron consisting of *Leander* and *Naiad* and the destroyers *Jaguar, Kingston*, and *Nizam* coming down from the north. (An additional four ships *Jervis, Havock, Hotspur*, and *Decoy* deployed further offshore on anti-submarine patrol.) As searchlights snapped on and began probing their location the French destroyers increased speed and turned south. *Valmy*'s captain remembered: "Shadows danced on the bridge. We exchanged brief words as the guns swiveled to compensate for our evasive

maneuvers. Then the sound of enemy artillery rang out on multiple oc-
taves, each sounding a unique chord as shells tore the air."[90]

As the French destroyers completed their turn, *Naiad*, only five thousand yards away, hit *Guépard*. The 5.25-inch round penetrated her after
magazine but failed to explode. In any case the magazine was empty as
her crew had landed *Guépard*'s ordnance just the day before. *Valmy* flung
two torpedoes at 0153. Then "at 0155, the action reached its climax: speed
was twenty-eight knots, communications with *Guépard* had broken down.
It was necessary to operate using our own judgment. Between the two destroyers there sprang up an orchard of geysers that immediately showered
orange stars. Searchlights perforated the night unceasingly."[91] *Leander*
launched four torpedoes and *Jaguar* two more. The French ships hugged
the coast so close that the British rounds sailing over exploded ashore and
set the shrub forest ablaze. At that moment *Guépard* and *Valmy* rounded
Cape Ras Beyrouth. French shore batteries opened fire in their support.
And then, as suddenly as it had begun, the action was over. De Lafond's
ships passed into the night without further damage. *Élan*, operating sepa-
rately ran aground trying to evade detection, but eventually worked her
way off and returned to Beirut.

This was the campaign's last surface action. On 25 June the submarine
HMS *Parthian* sank the submarine *Souffleur* off Beirut. The British continued to rotate ships in and out of the theater, giving crews a chance to
rest. More aircraft became available and the fleet began to enjoy support
from "real" fighters as opposed to the ineffective Fulmers. The stalemate
ashore finally began to breakup. On 3 July Palmyra fell while the Austral-
ians occupied Damur just south of Beirut on 10 July. With a rare victory in
the air morale began to rise. One of *Hotspur*'s officers recalled: "It a way
it was a pity to leave the Syrian coast. After Greece and Crete it was an
excellent tonic to be doing something aggressive again."[92] The French,
however, despite the looming specter of defeat, battled grimly on. Darlan
devised a scheme to send the battleship *Strasbourg* with four cruisers, a
division of destroyers and another of torpedo boats to transport four infan-

---

[90] Darrieus and Quéguiner, *Marine française*, 275.

[91] *Ibid.*

[92] Gill, 380.

try battalions to Syria. *Guépard*, *Valmy*, and *Vauquelin*, meanwhile, sailed to Salonika to embark a battalion that had arrived from France by rail. On 9 July British aircraft spotted the ships about two hundred miles from Syria on their return journey. According to orders and rather than risk the lives of hundreds of soldiers, they made for Toulon instead of Beirut. The French authorities finally asked for an armistice and the fighting ended by 14 July. Thus concluded what Admiral Cunningham described as "an irritating though necessary interlude in the midst of all our other commitments and responsibilities."[93] He noted that "encounters with the enemy's ships were definitely not satisfactory and it must be conceded that the honors rested with the French destroyers. This comparatively petty campaign absorbed the entire effort of all reconnaissance aircraft available for naval co-operation in the eastern Mediterranean, with the exception of those based on Malta. All reconnaissance to the west of Alexandria had to be stopped and 'Tobruk left wide open to surprise'. Even so, the available aircraft were insufficient for the Syrian operations."[94]

While Admiral Cunningham dismissed the campaign as an irritating interlude, it was, in fact, very significant. Mussolini had been casting covetous eyes upon Tunisia, but events in Syria demonstrated that Tunisia would not be an easy prize, especially with the entire French African Empire as its hinterland. Thus, Tunisia remained French as long as there was a French state. The campaign was more important, however, for what did not happen. If ever there was a moment when France stood on the verge of history it was in June 1941. On one side was partnership in the Axis, on the other a proud, but frustrated, neutrality. While it was true that by late June German attention was focused on Russia, the chiefs of the German air force and navy, Herman Göring and Erich Raeder, both promised their cooperation to *Strasbourg*'s proposed sortie. Admiral Darlan ultimately decided, once again, however, that all-out war with Britain was not in France's best interest. That he selected the wiser path history demonstrated as France emerged from the holocaust of the Second World War among the victors and one of the great powers. In June 1941 such a result seemed unimaginable.

---

[93] Cunningham, *Sailor's Odyssey*, 398.

[94] http://www.nzetc.org/tm/scholarly/tei-WH2Navy-c8.html

CHAPTER 7. THE ROAD BACK BEGAN AT BALIKPAPAN

The last weeks of January 1942 were dark indeed for the Allied forces confronting Japan's furious onslaught: Manila fallen, Burma invaded, Malaya overrun. But for Japan's war planners these victories just cleared the road to the real prize, the Dutch East Indies. Japan went to war to control this rich archipelago and, only five weeks into the conflict, the soldiers of the Rising Sun seemed poised to achieve their nation's goal.

The invasion began even as operations in Malaya and the Philippines continued. Vice Admiral Nobutake Kondo's Southern Force completely outmatched his American, British, Dutch and Australian opponents. He planned "an island-hopping, three-pronged simultaneous attack from the west, north and east, pointed at and converging on the island of Java."[95] The central thrust aimed at Borneo's oil-rich east coast. The quick and largely unopposed occupation of British Borneo on 16 December 1941, followed by the collapse of American resistance in the Philippines (except for Bataan) in early January 1942 set the stage for the central prong's advance.

On 7 January 1942 the 56th and 2nd Kure Special Naval Landing Force departed Davo on sixteen transports. Rear Admiral Shoji Nishimura commanding the 4th Destroyer Squadron, the 11th and 30th Minesweeper Divisions and the 31st Sub Chaser Division escorted this fleet.

Dutch aircraft spotted the Japanese convoy on 10 January. Although their exposed northern outpost had no realistic hope of repelling the attack, the Dutch garrison, a reinforced battalion, resisted for a day and shore batteries sank a pair of minesweepers just after noon on 12 January. The minelayer *Prins van Oranje,* 1,291 tons standard displacement, armed with a pair of 3-inch guns and capable of fifteen knots, attempted to escape that night, but while passing through the channel north of Tarakan Island, she ran afoul of patrol boat *P38* and the destroyer *Yamakaze* patrolling off-

---

[95] Japanese Monograph 101, 10.

shore. The Dutch ship fled, but at 2357, after an unequal fight, the Japanese warships sank her sixteen miles east of the island's northern point. Only sixteen members of *Prins van Oranje*'s crew survived.

The swift fall of Tarakan provided the Japanese with a forward airbase and, only four days after the Dutch surrender, they had fighters operating from the island's airstrip to cover the next leap forward. On 21 January fifteen transports and Nishimura's light cruiser, ten destroyers, three patrol boats, four minesweepers and four sub chasers, departed Tarakan bound for Balikpapan, a port and important oil center two thirds of the way down Borneo's east coast.

The brand new American British Dutch Australian (ABDA) command expected the Japanese and eagerly sought an opportunity to bring them to battle. However, a multi-national command structure, different languages, inadequate communication systems and personality conflicts crippled their efforts. One Dutch officer said of the ABDA headquarters: "nobody knew what anybody else was doing. You've never seen such a mixed-up thing as that headquarters."[96]

The United States Navy held responsibility for the eastern approaches to the Dutch East Indies and assembled there Task Force 5. This included the heavy cruiser USS *Houston*, the light cruisers USS *Boise* and USS *Marblehead*, and eight destroyers under Rear Admiral William A. Glassford. He led the light cruisers and six destroyers north on 17 January hoping to surprise a Japanese force reported off Kema, Celebes. When his intelligence proved faulty, Glassford returned south and rendezvoused with the *Houston* and two more destroyers at Kebola Bay, Sumbawa. The assembled captains of this relatively powerful force held a battle conference on 18 January in response to new intelligence of Japanese movements toward Balikpapan. "The air was supercharged with excitement."[97] But even before the meeting ended, American submarines reported the Japanese had failed to move as anticipated. The *Houston*'s reconstructed logs records:

---

[96] Schultz, *Last Battle Station*, 73.

[97] Winslow, *Ghost*, 61.

"In P.M. we were told the orders were cancelled. All growling for a fight. *Boise* and three cans going west. *Houston* and three cans east."[98]

On 20 January 20, Dutch army reports of the awaited Japanese advance down the Makassar Strait led Admiral Thomas Hart, commander of AB-DAFLOAT, the joint Allied Naval command, to order Glassford to make a third attempt to find and fight the elusive foe. The *Houston*, by that time, was escorting a convoy east of Darwin while the light cruisers and six destroyers of Task Force 5 lay refueling at Kupang, Timor. This task they hurriedly finished and that afternoon the American ships weighed anchor anticipating action and wondering if this, the third time, would prove the charm.

On 21 January, while navigating Sape Strait about a third of the way along the difficult eight hundred mile approach, the *Boise* tore a hole in her bottom on an uncharted pinnacle.[99] At this point Admiral Glassford could have justifiably aborted his mission, especially as word came in the initial sighting reports were false. Instead, he ordered Destroyer Division 59—USS *John D. Ford*, USS *Pope*, USS *Parrot*, and USS *Paul Jones* under Commander Paul H. Talbot aboard the *Ford*—to continue north to a patrol position off the Postillion Islands at the southern end of Makassar Strait while the *Boise* and *Marblehead* (she had burned out a turbine restricting her speed to fifteen knots) headed west toward Lombok Strait between Bali and Lombok.

On 22 January the submarine USS *Pike* reported twenty-six enemy ships escorted by fourteen destroyers advancing down Makassar Strait toward Balikpapan.[100] Finally, this was the hard intelligence the Americans should have waited for from the beginning. For the fourth time, Hart ordered Task Force 5 to attack. Glassford transferred his flag from *Boise* (she needed to have her damage inspected at Surabaya) to *Marblehead* and, picking up USS *Bulmer* (she was suffering from salting in her condensers) as an escort, he turned north to provide a rendezvous point about

---

[98] http://www.ibiblio.org/hyperwar/USN/ships/logs/CA/ca30.html#Encla11

[99] "It was a difficult passage through the Flores Sea, made no easier by the inaccuracy of the English-language charts. The Dutch charts were better, but none of the Americans could read them and the Dutch claimed they had no extra pilots available." Leutze, *A Different King of Victory*, 270.

[100] Blair, *Silent Victory*, 166.

a hundred miles south of Balikpapan for the four destroyers to fall back upon after their attack. By thrusting at shadows and using heavy warships as escorts in waters far outside the range of Japanese air and surface forces, Hart had reduced his punch from three cruisers and eight destroyers to only four destroyers.

Figure 50. *Sendai* class light cruiser underway 1924/25. At night in poor visibility the Japanese repeatedly mistook the U.S. destroyers for this class of vessel (US Navy)

The destroyers of Destroyer Division 59 began their long run north on the morning of 23 January. Talbot intended to arrive off Balikpapan two hours before dawn and execute a surprise torpedo attack. The weather in the straits helped his hopes of obtaining surprise. The destroyers ran through massive seas that broke green over their forward mounts and broke bridge windows and buckled spray shields aboard *Pope*. However, "as the column approached the lee shore of Balikpapan, the rain decreased and the seas changed to long, slow swells."[101] At 0200 hours as the Americans neared their target "the loom of gigantic fires became visible." The sailors "could smell burning oil 20 miles at sea." [102] A sailor aboard the *Pope* caught the mood: "the canopy of smoke hung over us, lending a si-

---

[101] Mullin, "Balikpapan, 1942." 18.

[102] Smith, 75.

nister touch to the proceedings. We seemed cut off from the rest of the world as we approached a misplaced corner of Hell."[103]

Figure 51. USS *Pope* (DD-225) steaming at speed. She participated in surface actions in January, February and March 1942. Japanese aircraft finally sank her south of Borneo while attempting to escape the Java Sea in company with HMS *Exeter* and HMS *Encounter* (US Navy)

The same storm system that buffeted Destroyer Division 59 screened the Japanese invasion convoy during most of its voyage. However, at 1525 nine Dutch B-10 bombers based at Samarinda found the fleet. Their attack damaged *Tatsugami Maru* (7,070 tons) and crippled *Nana Maru* (6,557 tons), which sank later. Nonetheless, the convoy arrived at 2045 hours and anchored in two rows; eight ships near the shore and the rest further out. The company-sized Dutch garrison had destroyed the oil storage tanks and torched the refinery before the Japanese started disembarking at 2130. The scene was spectral with flames casting a reddish glow against the underside of dark thunderheads and the winds blowing thick, greasy smoke southeast out to sea.

---

[103] Michel, *Mr. Michel's War*, 45.

At 2345 hours the Dutch submarine *K-XVIII*, attacking trimmed on the surface due to the weather, fired four torpedoes at Nishimura's flagship, the light cruiser *Naka*. This volley missed its target, but, continuing past, one 21-inch weapon struck *Tsuruga Mara* (6,987 tons).[104] This blow had the fateful effect of focusing Nishimura on the submarine threat as *Naka* and her ten destroyers fanned out to the northeast of the anchorage to hunt the attacker. The admiral left his smaller warships, three patrol boats, four minesweepers and three sub chasers patrolling back and forth around the anchored convoy.

Talbot's column had several close calls as it approached its target. At 0245 *Ford* reported a column of four enemy destroyers passing ahead from starboard to port. Talbot ignored a blue signal blinker flashed by the last ship and adjusted course slightly to starboard. Another witness aboard *Ford* remembered that: "a whole division of Jap destroyers burst out of the gloom and oil smoke on our port bow and steamed rapidly across in front of us and off into the darkness to starboard... I don't know why they didn't see us."[105] However, the old American destroyers bore a fortunate resemblance to *Naka* and the Japanese repeatedly mistook the American ships for friendly vessels.

The American ships, all vintage 1919, displaced 1,308 tons full load. They carried four 4-inch/51-caliber guns and a 3-inch antiaircraft gun. Four triple banks of torpedoes mounted two to a side made them potentially dangerous ship-killers. Theoretically they could reach thirty-two knots, but hard use and postponed maintenance made that speed wishful thinking. The Japanese patrol boats, *PC36, PC37,* and *PC38* were ex-destroyers of a similar type, launched in 1922 and displacing 1,162 tons. After their conversion they carried two 4.7-inch/45-caliber guns and were capable of eighteen knots. The minesweepers all had a pair of 4.7-inch/45-caliber guns. *W15* and *W16* launched in 1933, displaced 800 tons and streamed at eighteen knots. *W17* and *W18* launched in 1935, displaced 707 tons and could make nineteen knots. Nishimura's flotilla consisted of *Naka* (7,100

---

[104] She subsequently witnessed the American attack and at dawn unsuccessfully attacked the transports once again. *Ch12* counterattacked and inflicted non-fatal damage on the Dutch boat.

[105] Smith, 75. There were many Japanese ships crisscrossing through the area and with their high speed and given the intermittent visibility, the accounts differ on what ships the Americans encountered and when these encounters occurred.

tons, seven 5.5-inch 50-caliber guns, eight 24-inch torpedo tubes and thirty-five knots); Destroyer Division 2: *Yudachi, Samidare, Harusame*; Destroyer Division 9: *Asagumo, Murasame, Minegumo, Natsugumo*; and Destroyer Division 24: *Kawakaze, Yamakaze Umikaze*. The destroyers were modern, first line units, rated at thirty-four or thirty-five knots and armed with five or six 5-inch 50-caliber guns and eight 24-inch torpedo tubes with re-loads. They completely outmatched the elderly American "cans."

At 0245 hours *Ford*'s lookout reported transports about nine thousand yards off the port bow silhouetted periodically against the lurid fires burning ashore. Followed by *Pope, Parrott* and *Paul Jones* she closed range running northwest at twenty-seven knots. Then, *Ford* met "an enemy destroyer on opposite course which passed close to starboard."[106] This "destroyer", *W15*, proceeded to unwittingly play the part of red herring. According to her account she was "moving slowly in the northern part of the anchorage (and) sighted an unknown vessel which, because of its four funnels, was at first believed to be the flagship *Naka*, then supposed to be on patrol near the anchorage. After a second ship came in sight, the vessels were revealed as four-funneled enemy destroyers. Soon four enemy vessels closed in rapidly at a very high speed, passing at a very close range. Without attacking they disappeared."[107] In fact, the Americans did attack. The *Ford* snapped off one quick torpedo which missed astern. The *Pope* held her fire, unable to train her starboard tubes in time, but the *Parrott* fired five (two unintentionally, practically denuding her starboard batteries). Finally, at 0257 the *Jones*, at the end of the line, contributed another. The eager Americans squandered more than an eighth of their torpedo power on at a small target moving on a reciprocal course; this effectively defanged their initial attack because by 0300 Talbot saw he was running past the Japanese concentration and ordered a starboard turn to course 170 degrees for another try. As *Ford* came about, *Parrott*, tracking a target to port, launched three more torpedoes. At 0302 "there was a flash ahead of us, and a great mushroom of flame leaped hundred of feet into the air."[108] *Sumanoura Maru*, a transport displacing 3,519 tons blew up. *Ford*'s gunnery officer, William P. Mack remembered: "The explosion of a torpedo

---

[106] *Java Sea Campaign*, 19.

[107] Japanese Monograph No. 101, 27.

[108] Michel, 45.

at night at close range is an awe-inspiring sight. The blast is terrific, blinding; then comes the concussion wave, which leaves you gasping for breath."[109]

For the Japanese this marked the third attack that night; but *Sumanoura Maru*'s destruction, spectacular as it was, did not reveal the agent. At 0302 the Americans were beyond the anchorage embroiled in smoke streaming from the oil tanks. If *W15* had identified enemy four-stack destroyers, Nishimura never got the word. He blamed the blast on submarines and led his ships out to sea once again.

As the powerful Japanese escort chased phantoms, the four American destroyers steadied on a southerly course. At 0303 *Ford* and *Pope* each fired one torpedo at a "destroyer" abeam to starboard. At 0306 *Pope* noted a more promising target to starboard, a bunched group of ships signaling with blinkers. She replied with five torpedoes, emptying her starboard tubes. As they followed *Parrott* and *Paul Jones* each added another torpedo at 0308 and 0310 respectively. One torpedo from these salvoes struck *Tatsukami Maru*, an ammunition ship of 7,064 tons displacement. Her explosion lit the night. Meanwhile at 0309, *Pope* chipped a shot at a "destroyer" passing abeam to port, but missed.

At 0314 *Ford* led her three consorts on a hard swing to starboard to penetrate the southern end of the Japanese line. *Ford* shot a torpedo at a "destroyer" to port while at 0319 *Pope* and *Parrott* heading west emptied their tubes, firing five and three torpedoes respectively, at a "destroyer" less than two thousand yards to port. *Pope* reported two and the *Parrott* one explosion followed by a high column of smoke. In all cases, the target was probably *P37*. She sank in shallow water and, although raised later, she never returned to service. At 0322 *Paul Jones* discharged one torpedo at *Kuretake Maru* (5,175 tons) spotted underway about a thousand yards off her port beam. This missed but *Ford* led the column to port around her, first south and then back east and *Paul Jones* hit with one more torpedo fired at 0325.

---

[109] Smith, 76.

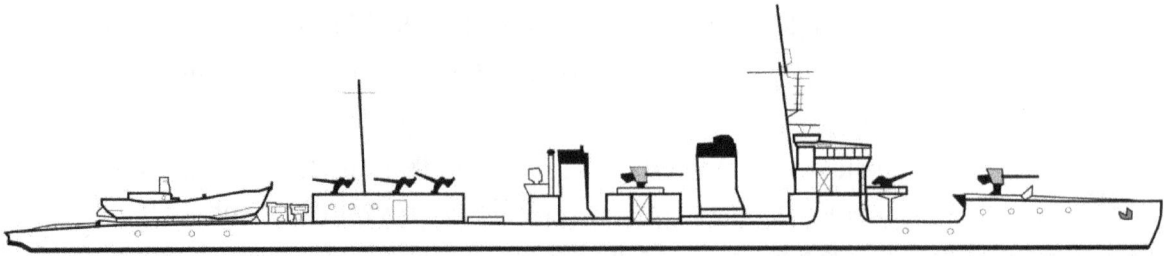

P37 ex *Hishi*

```
0                    25                   50
```
Meters   O'Hara - March 2005

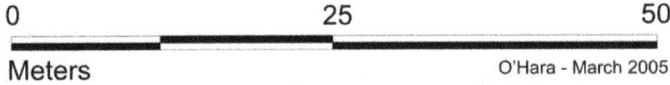

Figure 52. *P37*, a converted *Momi* class destroyer was the largest warship to
tangle with Destroyer Division 59 off Balikpapan. She lost her torpedo tubes
and one gun in her 1939 transformation to patrol boat. In 1941 she was further
modified to carry a Diahatsu landing craft (V. P. O'Hara)

Continuing the 360 degree swing around the stricken *Kuretake Maru*,
Ford led the column north. At 0325 *Pope* and *Parrott* began firing as targets flashed by to port although "due to maneuvers in column at high
speed it was difficult for guns to remain directed very long upon any one
target."[110] *Parrott* also got into the act and even fired star shell at 0330.
Although both ships claimed multiple hits on "destroyers" and transports,
the bright flashes of their gunfire made observation difficult. *Paul Jones*
fired a single torpedo at a target on her port beam at about this time. All
the "destroyers" the Americans encountered were patrol boats, sub chasers
or minesweepers ineffectively milling about. Despite high speed, intermit-
ted visibility and violent maneuvers, Destroyer Division 59 still maintained formation. This allowed the American captains to safely target any
vessel not in column.

---

[110] *Pope* Action Report, 3.

Figure 53. USS *John D. Ford*, DD228 was one of just four Asiatic Fleet destroyers to escape the debacle in the Dutch East Indies, slipping through Bali Strait on 1 March 1942. Her battle honors included Balikpapan, Badung Strait, and Java Sea. This view dates from August 1942. (US Navy)

At 0335 *Ford* turned northwest to pass through the first line of transports once again. The flagship passed "the smoking hulk of a merchant ship (*Nana Maru*) standing on end with lifeboats nearby."[111] Then at 0340 she sheered out of line to starboard suddenly concerned that a mine field lay ahead. This forced *Pope* to swerve to port to avoid a collision.[112] These radical maneuvers disrupted the column and the flagship quickly lost contact with the rest of her division. First *Parrott* and *Paul Jones* peeled off, circling back south and out of the action, followed shortly after by *Pope*.

The *Ford* still had torpedoes. Underway once again, she penetrated the inner line of transports and at 0346 fired her last two at *Tsuruga Maru*, *K-XVIII*'s victim of four hours earlier. The resulting explosion shook the American destroyer; then one minute later, *Asahi Maru* gained a measure of revenge landing a small caliber shell on *Ford*'s aft deckhouse, igniting an insignificant fire and wounding four men. This blow represented the only harm inflicted on the Americans. *Ford* circled back to the southeast to avoid running aground, her four inch guns firing as targets came in view. Mack wrote: "I didn't use any of the complicated fire-control apparatus installed ... as targets loomed out of the dark at ranges of 500 to

---

[111] *Java Sea Campaign,* 22.

[112] This is a controversial event. The version here is from *Ford*'s action report. Other accounts say it was shoal water, or a clogged boiler feed that caused the flagship's sudden change of course.

1,500 yards we trained on and let go a salvo or two, sights set at their lower limits."[113]

By 0400 *Ford* turned south to find her division and just in time. *Naka, Minegumo* and *Natsugumo*, finally suspecting the true nature of the attack, pursued briefly. By 0642 Destroyer Division 59 had reunited and at 0815 they joined *Marblehead* and *Bulmer*. The Japanese remained uncertain about what exactly had happened. Admiral Matome Ugaki's diary entry for 25 January noted: "In Balikpapan a special transport, a tanker and a patrol boat were damaged. It must have been due to enemy submarines and planes which sneaked in there."[114]

Figure 54. Nishimura's flagship Naka off Tarakan, January 1942. Attacked by a Dutch submarine, off Balikpapan, she led her destroyers on a wild goose chase while the Americans ran wild among the transports (http://users.kiss.si/~k4kt0234/japan%20(4).jpg)

Although Talbot's old warships clearly won a tactical victory in the first surface engagement fought by the United States Navy since the Spanish American War and the first victory achieved solely by warships against the Japanese, most historians think he should have done better. "Three [sic] four-pipers had run amuck through an anchored and silhouetted convoy, choosing their own range and time to fire torpedoes; yet even

---

[113] Smith, "Action off Balikpapan," 76.

[114] Ugaki, *Fading Victory*, 77.

the over-optimistic "score" of the morning after was disappointing."[115] Destroyer Division 59's "failure" is generally attributed to a lack of experience, a hasty approach and defective torpedoes. But theory is one thing and actual battle quite another. To what should the Battle of Balikpapan be compared? During the First Battle of Narvik five British destroyers surprised a harbor crowded with twenty-three merchant ships and five enemy destroyers. They filled the small anchorage with torpedoes and shellfire for an hour and ten minutes, attacking at slow speed one-by-one. Only two of the twenty-six torpedoes they fired struck a warship. The British enjoyed better visibility, a stationary foe and freedom from the threat of a far stronger escort (they did not realize five German destroyers lay at other anchorages around the long fjord). Still, only 7.6 percent of their torpedoes stuck their intended targets compared to (at least) 12.5 percent of the American torpedoes fired at Balikpapan.

The Battle of Balikpapan was a remarkable effort. The Americans slipped past a vastly superior escort, sank a quarter of the enemy transports with defective torpedoes and escaped unharmed. A year and a half would pass, filled with bitter and hard fought defeats, before American torpedoes fired from a destroyer would again damage Japanese ships. In fact, Balikpapan was a harbinger of things to come. It was the first in a long series of "small and savage actions, normally fought at night, among the islands of the South Pacific" that contributed to the slow, but steady destruction of Japanese naval power.[116] Truly the road back began at Balikpapan.

---

[115] Morison. *Rising Sun*, 290.
[116] Wilmott, *Empires in the Balance*, 291.

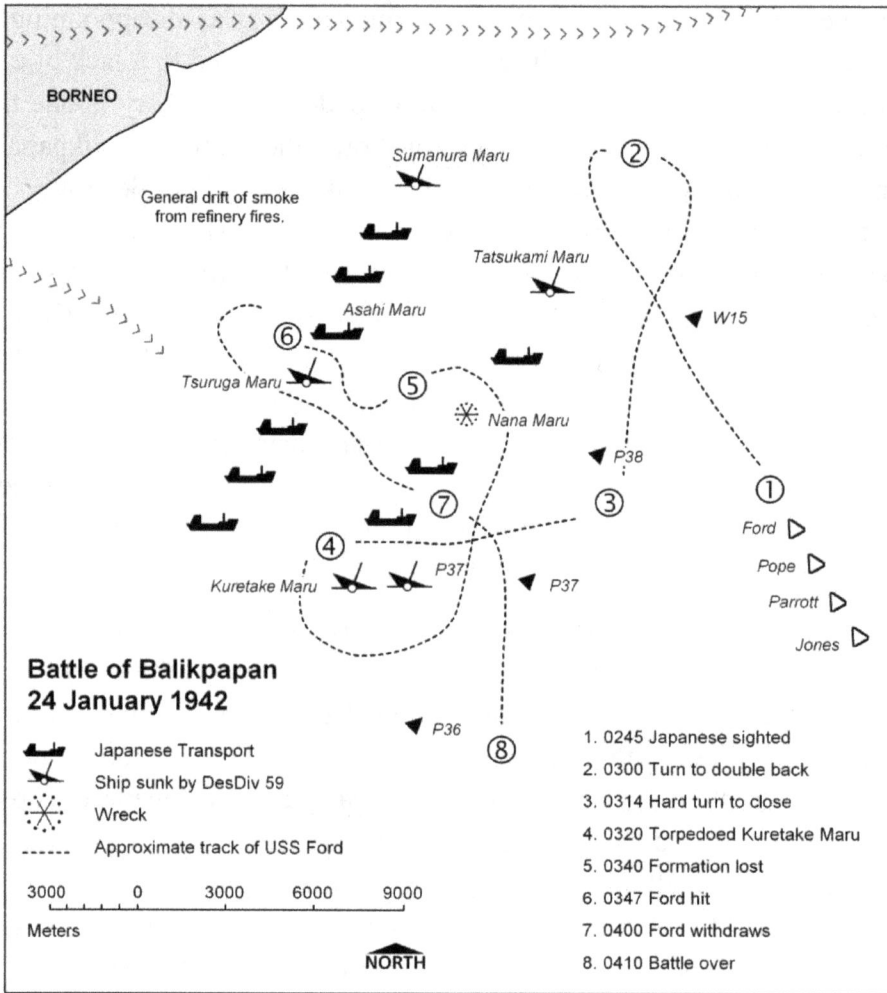

Figure 55. The Battle of Balikpapan, 24 January 1942. (V.P. O'Hara)

Figure 56. The spoils of victory. Japanese soldiers at Balikpapan celebrating a gusher. (http://users.kiss.si/~k4kt0234/japan%20(4).jpg)

BIBLIOGRAPHY

Agarossi, Elena. *A Nation Collapses, The Italian Surrender of September 1943*. Cambridge: Cambridge University Press, 2000.

Antier, Jean-Jacques. Les grandes Batailles Navales de la Seconde Guerre mondiale, Le drame de la Marine française. Paris: Ómnibus, 2001.

Ando, Elio. "The Gabbiano Class Corvettes Part 1 and Part 2". *Warship Volume IX*, 1985, 81-89 and 198-206.

Auphan, Paul and Jacques Mordal. *The French Navy in World War II*. Westport: Greenwood Press, 1976.

Bagnasco, Erminio and Enrico Cernuschi, *Le navi da guerra italiane 1940-1945*. Parma: Ermanno Albertelli Editore, 2003.

Barnett, Correlli. Engage the Enemy More Closely. The Royal Navy in the Second World War. London: W.W. Norton & Company, 1991.

Bernstein, Marc D. "Tin Cans Raid Balikpapan." *Proceedings*, April 2003, 80-83.

Blair, Clay, Jr. *Silent Victory*. New York, Bantam, 1976.

Bragadin, Antonio. *The Italian Navy in World War II*. Annapolis: Naval Institute Press, 1957.

Brown, David. *Warship Losses Of World War Two*. Annapolis: Naval Institute Press, 1995.

Bulkley, Robert J. Jr. *At Close Quarters: PT Boats in the United States Navy*. Annapolis: Naval Institute Press, 2003.

Calnan, Denis. "The *Saumarez* and the *Haguro*." Proceedings #788: October 1968, 147-150.

Cardea, Mario. "La Brillante Azione Della Torpediniera "Aliseo." *Mare - L'Italia Marinara*, pp. 1-5.

Carré, Paul. *Le Fantasque L'odyssée de la 10ᵉ DCL*. Nantes: Marines edition, 1994

Churchill, Winston S. *The Second World War Volume III, The Grand Alliance*, Houghton Mifflin: Boston, 1950.

Cocchia, Aldo. *The Hunters and the Hunted*. New York: Arno Press, 1980.

Combined Operations Web Site:
http://www.combinedops.com/Black%20Hackle.htm

Cooper, Bryan. *The Battle of the Torpedo Boats*. New York: Stein and Day, 1970.

Cruickshank, Charles, *The German Occupation of the Channel Islands*. London: Oxford University Press, 1975.

Cunningham, Andrew Browne. *A Sailor's Odyssey*. London: Hutchinson, 1951.

Darlington, Robert and Fraser McKee. *The Canadian Naval Chronicle 1939-1945*. St. Catharines: Vanwell, 1998.

Darrieus, Amiral Henri and Jean Queguiner. *Historique de la Marine française 1922-1942*. St Malo: l'Ancre de Marine, 1996.

Dear, I. C. B., ed.. *The Oxford Companion to World War II*. Oxford: Oxford University Press, 1995.

DePalma, Arthur R. "Japanese Naval Nightmare." *World War II*, Feb 2001, Vol. 15/6, 50-56.

Dull, Paul S. *A Battle History of the Imperial Japanese Navy* (1941-1945). Annapolis: Naval Institute Press, 1982.

Eisenhower, Dwight D.. *Crusade in Europe*. New York: Doubleday & Company, 1948.

Freivogel, Zvonimir. "Siluranti ex Italiane Sotto Bandiera Tedesca." *Storia Militare*, September 1996, 18-29 and October 1996, 22-35.

Gardiner, Robert, ed. Conway's All the World's Fighting Ships 1922-1946. New York: Mayflower 1980.

Gill, G. Hermon. *Royal Australian Navy 1939-1942*. Adelaide: Griffin Press, 1957.

Greene, Jack and Alessandro Massignani. *The Black Prince and the Sea Devils*. (Cambridge, MA: Da Capo Books, 2004).

Gröner, Erich. *German Warships 1815-1945, Volume II*. London: Conway Maritime Press, 1991.

Guiglini, Jean. "A Resume of the Battle of Koh-Chang, 17 January 1941," *Warship International* 2/1990 , K.R. Macpherson, translator.

Gwynn-Jones, Terry. "Forgotten Air War Over Indochina." *Aviation History*, September 2000.

Hackett, Bob and Sander Kingsepp. *Junyokan TROM Haguro.* http://www.combinedfleet.com/haguro_t.htm

Harker, Jack S. *Well Done Leander*. Auckland: Collins, 1971.

Hawkins, Ian, Ed. *Destroyer, An Anthology of First-Hand Accounts of the War at Sea 1939-1945*. London: Conway Maritime Press, 2003.

Heckstall-Smith, *The Fleet that Faced Both Ways*. London: Anthony Blond, 1963.

Hervieux, Pierre. "German Auxiliaries at War 1939-45: Minesweepers, Submarine Chasers and Patrol Boats." *Warship 1995*, London: Conway Maritime Press, 1995.

—-. "German Type 45, 40 and 43 Minesweepers at War." *Warship 1996*. London: Conway Maritime Press, 1996.

Hinsley, F. H. British *Intelligence in the Second World War*. London, HMSO, 1993.

Hough, Stan. *HMS* Vigilant *1944 to 1946*.
http://homepage.ntlworld.com/stan.hough/Vigilant.htm

Jentschura, Hansgeorg, Dieter Jung and Peter Mickel. *Warships of the Imperial Japanese Navy, 1869-1945*. Annapolis: Naval Institute Press, 1986.

Langtree, Christopher. *The Kellys: British J, K & N Class Destroyers of World War II*. Annapolis: Naval Institute Press, 2002.

Lacroix, Eric and Linton Wells II. *Japanese Cruisers of the Pacific War*. Annapolis: Naval Institute Press, 1997.

Le Sauteur, Philip Frederick. *Jersey Under the Swastika*. http://tonylesauteur.com/arbre39.htm.

Leutze, James. *A Different Kind of Victory, a Biography of Admiral Thomas C. Hart*. Annapolis, Naval Institute Press, 1981.

Lott Arnold S., *Most Dangerous Sea: A History of Mine Warfare*. (Annapolis: U.S. Naval Institute, 1959), 17.

Lovatto, Alberto. "In Corsica doppo l'8 de settembre, Il Diario di Giovanni Milanetti." *L'impegno*, December 1996.

Mack, William P. "Macassar Merry-Go-Round" in *United States Navy in World War II*. New York, Quill, 1966, pg 73-78.

Manley, David. "The Battle of Koh Chang." http://www.btinternet.com/~david.manley/naval/genquar/kohchang.htm (last accessed 27 February 2011).

Michel, John, J. A. *Mr. Michel's War*. Novato, CA: Presidio, 1998.

Melka, Robert L. "Darlan between Britain and Germany 1940-41." *Journal of Contemporary History*. (April 1973).

Morison, Samuel Eliot. *History Of United States Naval Operations In World War II, The Rising Sun in the Pacific*. Boston: Little, Brown and Company, 1984.

—-. Volume IX, *Sicily-Salerno-Anzio*. Boston: Little Brown, 1990.

—-. Volume XI, *The Invasion of France and Germany*. Boston: Little, Brown, 1975.

Mullin, Daniel J. "Balikpapan, 1942". *Shipmate*, January-February 1984: 18-20.

Nevitt, Allyn. "Long Lancers TROM Kamikaze." http://www.combinedfleet.com/kamika_t.htm

Office of Naval Intelligence. *The Java Sea Campaign*. Washington DC: Navy Department, 1943

O'Hara, Vincent P. *The German Fleet at War 1939-1945*. Annapolis: Naval Institute Press, 2004.

—-. *Struggle for the Middle Sea: The Great Navies at War in the Mediterranean* Annapolis: Naval Institute Press, 2009.

—-. *The U.S. Navy against the Axis: Surface Combat 1941-1945*. Annapolis: Naval Institute Press, 2007.

Page, Christopher, ed. *The Royal Navy and the Mediterranean Volume II: November 1940-December 1941*. London: Frank Cass, 2002.

Pertek, J. *Wielkie dni malej floty*. Poznan: 1990.

Peszke, Michael Alfred, *Poland's Navy 1918-1945*. New York: Hippocrene Books, 1999.

Piaskowski, J. *Kroniki PMW*.

Pignato, N. and Cappellano, F.. "L'Esercito italiano dall'armistizio al trattato di pace Parte 1." *Storia Militare*, April 2001, pp. 45-57.

Reynolds, Leonard, C. *Dog Boats at War, Royal Navy D Class MTBs and MGBs 1939-1945*. Phoenix Mill: Sutton, 2000.

Roberts, Stephen S. "The Thai Navy." *Warship International* 3/1986

Roche, Jean Michel. La bataille de Koh Chang. www.netmarine.net/bat/croiseur/ lamotte/kohchang. Last accessed 25 February 2011.

Rohwer, J. and Hummelchen, G.. *Chronology of the War at Sea 1939-1945*. Annapolis: Naval Institute Press, 1992.

Roscoe, Theodore. *United States Destroyer Operations in World War II.* Annapolis: Naval Institute Press, 1953.

Roskill, Stephen. *The War at Sea 1939-1945, Volume III: The Offensive Part II.* Nashville: The Battery Press, 1994.

—-*White Ensign, The British Navy at War 1939-1945.* Annapolis: Naval Institute Press, 1966.

Ruge, Friedrich. "German Minesweepers in World War II." *Proceedings 595* (September 1952): 995-1003.

Sandel, Percy, Lieutenant. "Action Report, *PC-564*," 16 March 1945, National Archives II, College Park, MD.

—-. "Statement." 10 March 1945. National Archives II, College Park, MD.

Schull, Joseph. *Far Distant Ships, An Official Account of Canadian Naval Operations in World War II.* Toronto: Stoddart, 1991.

Scott, Peter. *The Battle of the Narrow Sea.* London: Country Life, 1945.

Showell, Jak P. Mallmann. *Fuehrer Conferences on Naval Affairs 1939-1945.* London: Chatham Publishing, 2005.

Smith, N. E. "Action off Balikpapan, N.E.I, Morning of January 24, 1942 – report of." USN Action Report, 1942.

Smith, Peter C. *Hold the Narrow Sea, Naval Warfare in the English Channel 1939-1945.* Ashbourne: Moorland Publishing, 1984.

Tarrant, V.E. *The Last Year of the Kriegsmarine.* Annapolis: Naval Institute Press, 1994.

Tapasanan, Vidya, correspondence based on information in: *Navikasart* (Naval Science) Magazine, March, 1993, February 1994, February 1995, published monthly by the Royal Thai Naval Institute, Royal Thai Navy.

—-.Royal Thai Navy. *Prawat Kongthap Rue Thai* (History oft he Royal Thai Navy), Naval Administration Department: Bangkok, 1976.

——.Royal Thai Navy Museum, Pak Nam

Tent, James F. *E-Boat Alert, Defending the Normandy Invasion Fleet*. Annapolis: Naval Institute Press, 1996.

Thomas, Martin. "After Mers-el-Kebir: The Armed Neutrality of the Vichy French Navy 1940-1943." *The English Historical Review* (June 1997).

Thompson, Julian. *The War at Sea, The Royal Navy in the Second World War*. Osceola: Motorbooks International, 1996.

Tomblin, Barbara Brooks. *With Utmost Spirit: Allied Naval Operations in the Mediterranean*. (Lexington, KY: University of Kentucky Press, 2004).

Ugaki, Matome. *Fading Victory*. Pittsburgh: University of Pittsburgh Press, 1991.

United States Army. *Netherlands East Indies Naval Invasion Operations*. Japanese Monograph No. 101. 1953.

——. Tarakan Invasion Operations Record. Japanese Monograph No 28.

USS *Gleaves*. "Action Report: Dragoon Operation: Invasion of Southern France." 13 October 1944.

USS *Brooklyn*. "Action Report, Operation Dragoon 11 September 1944 to 16 October 1944." 13 November 1944.

USS *Pope*. "Night Destroyer Attack off Balikpapan, January 24, 1942."

USS *Gleaves*. "Report of Surface Actions with German Forces, Night of October 1-2, 1944, 3 October 1944," USS *Gleaves* War Diary October 1-31, 1944, 31 October 1944.

USS *Gleaves*. "Capture of Enemy Personnel and Vessel, Report of." 3 October 1944.

Van Oosten, F. C. *The Battle of the Java Sea*. Annapolis: Naval Institute Press, 1976.

Vascotto, Vezio. "La battaglia di Koh Chang." *Storia Militare*, (149) February 2006, 16-24.

Von Gartzen, Wirich. *Die Flottille Außergewöhnlicher Seekrieg deutscher Mittelmeer-Torpedoboote.* (Hamburg: Koehlers Verlagsgesells, 1990)

Von Senger und Etterlin, Frido. *Neither Fear Nor Hope.* New York: E. P. Dutton, 1964.

War Diaries. "Kriegstagebuch Seetransportstelle Bastia." 9 September–4 October 1943. Facsimile.

—-. "Kriegstagebuch Seetransportstelle Italien." 9 September 1943. Facsimile.

—-. SKL, 1 October 1944 (courtesy of Peter M. Kreuzer)

Waters, S.D. *The Royal New Zealand Navy.* http://www.nzetc.org/etexts/WH2Navy.html.

Whitley, M.J. *Cruisers of World War Two.* Annapolis: Naval Institute Press, 1995.

—-. *Destroyers of World War Two.* Annapolis: Naval Institute Press, 1998.

Wilmott, H.P. *Empires in the Balance.* Annapolis: Naval Institute Press, 1982.

——. *Grave of a Dozen Schemes, British Naval Planning and the War Against Japan, 1943-1945.* Annapolis: Naval Institute Press, 1996.

Winslow, W. G. *The Fleet the Gods Forgot.* Annapolis: Naval Institute Press, 1994.

Winton, John. *Sink the Haguro! The Last Destroyer Action of the Second World War.* London: Seeley, Service & Co., 1979.

—-. *The War at Sea – The British Navy in World War II.* New York: William Morrow, 1968.

Wood, Alan and Mary. *Islands in Danger, The Story of the German Occupation of the Channel Islands 1940-1945.* London: Evan Brothers, 1956.

Wyatt, David K. *Thailand A Short History.* New Haven, CT, Yale University Press, 1982.